CAPE
WINELANDS
in style

Photography by David Rogers
Text by Wendy Toerien

AFRICA
Geographic

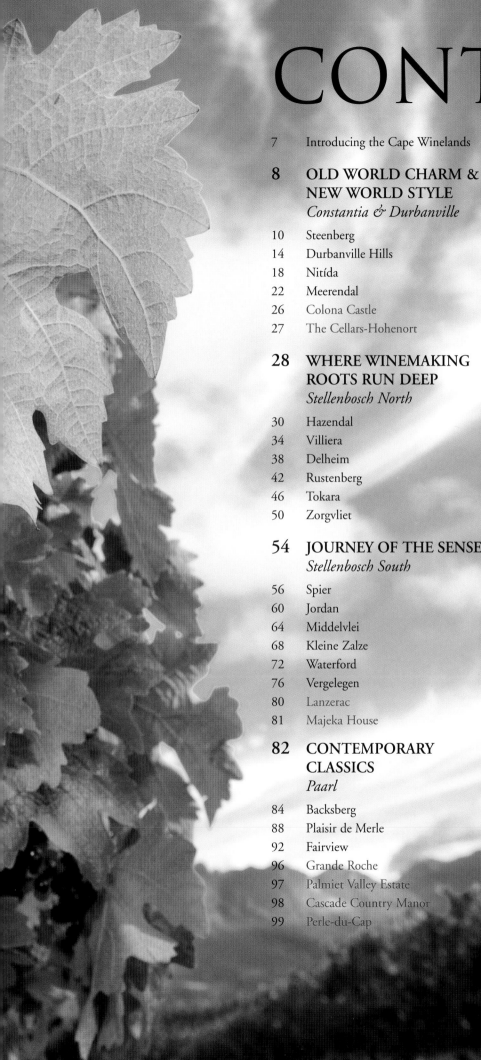

CONTENTS

Something Sweet
marinated
strawberries with
homemade ice cream
& shortbread
— R32 —

introducing
THE CAPE WINELANDS

The Cape, we think, boasts the most beautiful landscapes of all the wine-producing regions in the world. The Cape winelands have gentle hills and sea views in Constantia and Durbanville and great mountain peaks dominating Stellenbosch and Paarl. They stretch from Elgin's timberline near the coast to the rugged scrub of the interior around Robertson. And they encompass widely differing valleys: lush and green Franschhoek; extreme Tulbagh, with its summer heat and winter snow; and beautiful Hemel-en-Aarde, where vines share space with fragrant fynbos.

Winemaking has been a colourful thread in the fabric of local life since the first Dutch settlers arrived in Table Bay in 1652. On 2 February 1659, Cape Commander Jan van Riebeeck recorded in his journal: 'Today, God be praised, wine has been pressed for the first time from the grapes of the Cape.' In 2009, 350 years later, wine farms celebrate this proud tradition. We introduce a special selection of them here.

More than in any other leading New World wine-producing country – Australia, New Zealand, the USA, Argentina or Chile – winemaking in South Africa has been strongly influenced by the culture of the Old World. Historically, the classic grape varieties and wine styles of France and Germany held sway. But in recent decades South African wine has begun to establish its own distinctive identity, keeping pace with the country's acquisition of political independence and democracy and the deregulation of international trade and industry. Well-qualified, widely travelled viticulturists and winemakers are embracing the Cape's Mediterranean climate. They're exploring new areas, identifying the finest viticultural soils and coolest slopes, and planting the varieties that do best. They're combining simple, hands-on, age-old winemaking ways with ultra-sophisticated technological aids. And they're following sustainable farming principles in vineyard and winery through active environmental conservation and the social upliftment of farm workers and their communities. And the result? Wines of top quality in styles that straddle the New and Old Worlds: naturally fruit-rich and powerful, but nurtured with elegance and classicism in mind.

The Cape's return to the global wine stage has not only brought its wines international accolades, but also inspired its vintners to embrace wine tourism, combining sophistication with warm country hospitality. Visit beautifully restored Cape Dutch manor houses and see cellars that are centuries old or avant-garde architectural masterpieces. Taste world-class wine in a chic glass-walled space overlooking a hi-tech production facility or by candlelight over a simple wooden barrel. Eat at the tables of acclaimed chefs or picnic under camphor trees. Stay in a luxuriously restored 18th-century Cape Dutch manor house and appreciate art among the vines or receive a grape-skin spa treatment. Watch a bride arrive to say her vows in a converted cellar chapel; or hike a pristine patch of fynbos bordering vineyards. A glass of wine is simply the start of a varied and wonderful journey…

OLD WORLD CHARM

Constantia and Durbanville

The winelands of Constantia and Durbanville share more than just their conveniently close proximity to Cape Town. Their elegant, fruit-rich wines come from grapes grown on hillside vineyards with views over the cold Atlantic Ocean, providing the ideal cool, maritime climate for exceptional quality. But, whereas gracious Constantia is the historical heart of winemaking in the Cape, bottling world-renowned wines since the mid-18th century, Durbanville is the relatively new kid on the block. Vines have long been part of this rural community's farming activities, but it's only in modern times that its hospitable vintners have thrown open their cellar doors to visitors.

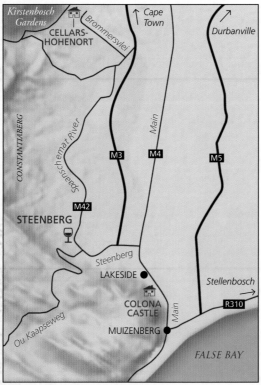

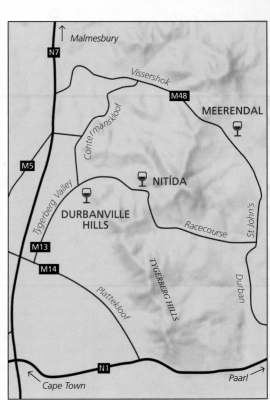

& NEW WORLD STYLE

STEENBERG

Constantia

More than three centuries ago, wine was being made at Steenberg

and weary travellers were offered humble board and lodging. Little has

changed, except that today the accommodation is far from humble.

Steenberg's cool-climate vineyards have been producing outstanding wines, particularly under progressive young winemaker John Loubser

In the early 1700s the Cape's Dutch colonial authorities decided that sheltered Simon's Bay, on the False Bay side of the Cape Peninsula, would make a better main harbour for the settlement than storm-buffeted Table Bay. It took two days to travel from Simon's Bay to Cape Town by ox wagon and horse-drawn carriage, and the farm Swaeneweide ('swans' feeding place') at the foot of Steenberg ('stone mountain') was exactly half way. So the farm's owner, widow Christina Diemer, started offering board and lodging – and, no doubt, wine with the meal, as it was her late husband Frederik Russouw who made the first wine here. He had bought the farm from a Cape legend, the indomitable Catharina Ras who, in 1682, had boldly asked Governor Simon van der Stel for land in Constantia, the cradle of Cape winemaking.

Physical reminders of the early entrepreneurs can be encountered at the farm today. The 'swans' that inspired Steenberg's original name – probably spur-winged geese or African sacred ibises – still visit the farm dams, and the 'holbol' gable added by Nicolaas Russouw still adorns the 18th-century manor house, now part of a five-star hotel. Several restored farm buildings are today's hotel suites, where furnishings and décor reflecting Western European and Dutch East Indian influences on the early Cape Colony have been combined with ultra-modern conveniences. Also part of this layout is the original cellar, stylishly renovated to house Catharina's Restaurant. At this top local venue for fine dining you will find executive chef Garth Almazan, who is known for his creative take on contemporary Cape cuisine.

Much of the development of Steenberg as a residential golf and wine estate was carried out in the 1990s by giant Johannesburg mining house Johnnic. A modern winery was built and some 60 hectares of vineyards were replanted with classic varieties by renowned Constantia viticulturist Herman Hanekom. Since then, Steenberg's cool-climate vineyards have been producing outstanding wines, particularly under progressive young winemaker John Loubser when the leisure and travel group Mantis Collection owned the estate. When Graham Beck bought the winery and hotel in 2005 Loubser, having worked at Beck's Robertson wine farm, expressed his pleasure with the comment, 'It's great to be making wine for a wine man again.'

Fine-tuning by the new owners included a revamp of Catharina's, opening it up to the surrounding views of lush Merlot vineyards, the nearby Silvermine mountains and distant False Bay. Furnishings are luxurious, but muted in earthy shades, with splashes of colour provided by contemporary artworks from the Becks' private collection – don't let your meal cool while you get a closer look at a vibrant Cecil Skotnes! You'll also know you're on a Beck property when you spot one of several Edoardo Villa sculptures artfully placed in unexpected spots – even the middle of a vineyard.

More substantial changes are being made at the tasting area of the cellar, where restyling includes a bistro overlooking the fermentation cellar, with a 'raw bar' for such specialities as steak tartare, oysters, sushi and sashimi. An upstairs room will cater for private, winemaker-led tastings as well as meetings and functions, while decks for alfresco tastings and dining will lead onto slopes planted to fragrant indigenous plants.

The emphasis on dining speaks of the new owners' understanding of Steenberg wines as accompaniments to food, with their distinctive minerality and classic dry tannins. Dictated by the lean, granite soils of the Stone Mountain slopes, these qualities are most evident in the two flagship wines: the Catharina red blend and the Magna Carta white blend, which features Steenberg's great Sauvignon Blanc and Sémillon.

Lida, who runs the tasting room, is a mine of information on all things vinous – ask her about the theory behind the Merlot's distinctive eucalyptus aroma. As you sample Steenberg wines, look around and you'll see what makes the farm so special: the vineyards, its *raison d'être* for 300 years.

PREVIOUS SPREAD Tasting room manager Lida van Heerden is a mine of information on Steenberg and its wines.

Steenberg Hotel's suites are in restored Cape Dutch buildings among the vineyards.

THIS SPREAD Accommodation offers modern comfort in traditional surroundings.

Catharina's combines elegance with warmth.

A new barrel is readied for filling in the underground cellar.

The 17th-century manor house features a convex-concave 'holbol' gable design, the only remaining example in the Cape.

Alfresco dining among the Merlot vines.

Don't miss... tasting Steenberg Nebbiolo, an Italian variety whose delicate fruit and dry finish will be recognised by European visitors, 'but may be strange to local palates,' says the winemaker. 'It reminds most, perhaps, of Pinot Noir.'

details

🍷 **Wine tasting/sales:** Mon-Fri 9 am-4.30 pm, Sat/Sun and public holidays 10 am-4 pm. Closed Easter Sunday, 25 December and 1 January. Tasting cost: Klein Steenberg and Premium wines – no charge (but R20 for groups larger than 10); Flagship and Icon wines – R50 (refunded on purchase).

🛢 **Cellar tours:** by appointment, tel. (+27-21) 713 2211.

🍽 **Restaurant:** Catharina's, open daily 7 am-10 pm; tel. (+27-21) 713 2222.

🏠 **Accommodation:** five-star Steenberg Hotel, tel. (+27-21) 713 2222.

ⓘ **In addition:** Steenberg Golf Course (preferential rates for hotel guests); tel. (+27-21) 713 2222. The Spa at Steenberg, operated by Ginkgo Spa & Wellness Group; tel. (+27-21) 713 2222.

☎ **Tel.** (+27-21) 713 2211.

🖱 **Website:** *www.steenberg-vineyards.co.za/ www.steenberghotel.com*

DURBANVILLE HILLS *Durbanville*

A tour of this impressive hill-top winery is a must, offering insight into the hi-tech world of winemaking, with magnificent views of the Cape Peninsula to match.

A visit to the ultra-modern concrete-and-stone Durbanville Hills winery is an awe-inspiring experience. Riding high on a hill like a ship on a sea of vineyards, the cellar represents a new way of winemaking in South Africa: combining private enterprise with corporate expertise to make and sell wines in generous quantities as well as limited-edition parcels.

Durbanville Hills sources all its grapes from the immediate vicinity, and in doing so is very much a community project. For years, a handful of local growers watched their top-quality grapes and wines disappear into the best-selling brands of large wine producers. Finally, in the late 1990s, they came to an arrangement with the wine and spirits giant Distell. The company built the ultra-sophisticated cellar on land belonging to one of the participating farmers while they, now shareholders, guaranteed the winery their combined crop.

A guided tour through the cellar gives you some idea of the remarkable scale of this enterprise. From the restaurant, a passage leads to massive glass doors that open onto a mezzanine-level walkway. Here you're in the company of giants: two connecting double-height cellars house row upon row of large, stainless steel fermentation tanks. They are extraordinary – as are the figures that go with them. There are 250 of these tanks and their individual capacities range from 6000 to 100 000 litres. Together they hold enough wine to fill nearly two million bottles. Downstairs, the maturation cellar is stacked with 2000 barrels of French and American oak, each with a capacity of 300 litres.

The grapes used are handpicked from about 770 hectares of vines. Sauvignon Blanc and Merlot are specialities, and the current range includes the single vineyard Biesjes Craal

Sauvignon Blanc, Luipaardsberg Merlot and Caapmans, a Cabernet Sauvignon/Merlot blend, all limited release wines only made in exceptional years. The Rhinofields range comprises a reserve line-up of three single-varietal wines (a Sauvignon Blanc, a Chardonnay and a Merlot) from no more than three separate vineyards. Apart from these, the bulk of the wine comes from the member farms and is blended for the Durbanville Hills range of wines. About 30 per cent of the winery's production goes overseas, to the United States, Canada and, more recently, New Zealand.

Juggling the different facets of this huge operation is experienced cellarmaster Martin Moore, who has been at Durbanville Hills since the cellar was completed in time for the winery's first harvest in 1999. He is assisted by two specialist winemakers: one for white wines and the other for red. An expert on traditional South African food, Moore specialises in matching his wines with exotic recipes for *potjiekos* (meat and vegetables slow-cooked in a cast-iron pot over an open fire), and he is never happier than when contributing to the winery's festive harvest days.

Pairing wine and local cuisine is an exercise you can try too, in the spacious, high-ceilinged @ The Hills restaurant. The knowledgeable staff will happily recommend an appropriate wine for biltong and blue cheese soup, for example, or ostrich medallions in a traditional sauce, and even crème brûlée made with Distell's best-selling Amarula fruit liqueur. White linen and dark furnishings against the backdrop of a crimson sunset and the lights of Cape Town make for elegant evening dining, yet children are welcome here too, especially on Sundays when a lavish buffet lunch is served.

Leading off the restaurant is the Bastion with a magnificent 180-degree sweep from Table Mountain across Table Bay to Robben Island and beyond. The design of this lookout point is based on the stone bastions of the 17th-century Castle of Good Hope in Cape Town, the country's oldest building. Enjoy the view, but hang on to your hat. It's almost always breezy, with winds coming from all directions – and helping to make Durbanville such a fine cool-climate wine region.

Don't miss... an opportunity to experience festive family harvest days in February and March, with sunset concerts on the lawns, special wine tastings, vineyard treasure hunts for the kids and other activities.

a crimson sunset and the lights of Cape Town make for elegant evening dining

PREVIOUS SPREAD The Durbanville Hills member farmers are shareholders in the winery, supplying cellarmaster Martin Moore (sitting, left) with top-quality grapes.

An early 18th-century Dutch ship's cannon, in full working order and on the same site where it was once mounted to signal farmers about the arrival of ships in Table Bay some 250 years ago.

THIS SPREAD The striking Durbanville Hills cellar sits proudly atop a series of rolling hills that overlook Table Mountain and Table Bay.

The tasting room.

The impressive maturation cellar holds some 2000 French and American oak barrels.

Large-scale photographs trace the winemaking process.

See glorious sunsets over Table Mountain from the Bastion leading off the restaurant.

details

🍷 **Wine tasting/sales:** Mon-Fri 9 am-4.30 pm; Sat and publc holidays 9.30 am-2.30 pm. Closed Easter Friday and Sunday, 25 and 26 December, 1 January. Tasting cost: R10.

🛢 **Cellar tours:** R20.

🍽 **Restaurant:** @ The Hills. Tel. (+27-21) 558 1337.

🍴 **Functions:** wedding receptions, conferences and seminars.

👪 **Children:** welcome, but no special provision made.

ⓘ **In addition:** special annual events, including wine and food pairing dinners, harvest day festivals, regional Sauvignon Blanc celebration, sunset concerts.

☎ **Tel:** (+27-21) 558 1300.

🖱 **Website:** *www.durbanvillehills.co.za*

NITÍDA
Durbanville

This boutique family wine farm celebrates the bounty of nature

like no other. Come and have fun with family and friends at

what has become the heart of a vibrant rural community.

Against a hillside in Durbanville Kloof, and barely visible among pines and bluegum trees, lies the gem that is Nitída. Named after *Protea nitida*, a plant found on the property, this wine farm is truly 'boutique' – the smallest cellar in this valley of wine farms. After nearly two decades, the owner himself still tends his vines and handcrafts his wines, albeit it with the assistance of a winemaker.

Bernhard Veller was a metallurgist in Gauteng before he moved to the Cape with his wife Peta towards the end of the 1980s. They came to Maasspruit farm in rural Durbanville, then still one of the Cape's best-kept viticultural secrets. Fired by an entrepreneurial spirit and a great love of wine, particularly red, Bernhard was soon bitten by the winemaking bug. When viticulturists confirmed that the farm's deep and rich, clay-based Hutton soils had potential for vines, he started planting in 1992, gradually building up to some 15 hectares of classic varieties: Sauvignon Blanc, Cabernet Sauvignon, Cabernet Franc, Merlot and Shiraz, as well as the Cape's home-grown Pinotage.

At the time, Bernhard was one of the first independent wine farmers in a valley with a history of grape growing that stretched back to the early 1700s. In the 20th century, Durbanville was an important yet little-known source of top-class fruit for some of the best-selling wine brands made by the large Cape wine wholesalers. Only four farms – Altydgedacht, Diemersdal, Bloemendal and Meerendal – were selling their own wines when he arrived. Self-taught and unencumbered by tradition, he kept his cellar small and his wine-making simple, focusing on modern scientific viticulture and matching specific varieties to the sites they were best suited to. Typically of Durbanville, the hills of his farm offer various different aspects, altitudes and micro-climates to produce the outstanding fruit he believed would sell his wines. In addition,

After a morning or afternoon of tasting, enjoy a meal at Cassia, the contemporary restaurant at the entrance to the farm

Don't miss... Nitída Degustazione, a farmers' market held on the last Saturday of each month where locals sell fresh produce of all kinds, including home-baked goods. On special weekends pre-ordered picnics can be enjoyed to the accompaniment of live music.

PREVIOUS SPREAD Peta Veller hosts delightfully convivial tastings in the barrel room.

Chic Cassia Restaurant specialises in contemporary, eclectic dishes.

THIS SPREAD Pincushion flowers in full bloom are more readily sighted than the *Protea nitida* which occurs naturally on the farm's hills.

Nitída's Degustazione farmers' market is a festive family affair.

Bernhard and Peta Veller surrounded by staff and children on the old farm tractor.

Fine dining on Cassia's dam-side sundeck.

Early-morning mists caress hillside vines about to bud.

the Southeaster, blowing in from the chilly Atlantic in summer, slows the ripening of the fruit and concentrates flavour in the berries.

A fermentation cellar, with a small collection of stainless steel tanks for the 140 tons of grapes harvested each year, is housed in a simple, sand-coloured building. In a similar building next door lie rows of small French oak barrels, in which Bernhard matures his red wines. At one end of it, at two counters sculpted from massive yellowwood trunks, you can sample Nitída's wines as you look out through the big wooden cellar doors down into the valley.

Durbanville has become renowned for its Sauvignon Blanc wines and Nitída's is one of the finest: a fresh, racy number full of tropical fruit flavours. The maiden 1995 vintage had connoisseurs sitting up and taking enough notice to award it a Veritas Double Gold. Bernhard has also started combining it with his award-winning Sémillon to produce a classic white Bordeaux-style blend called Coronata. Among the reds, a Pinotage earns its fair share of accolades too, although the smooth, full-fruited Calligraphy, a red blend made in the Bordeaux style, is considered the flagship. 'We are completely in love with our beautiful, elegant, cool-climate Cabernet,' says Bernhard. And, having replanted all the farm's virus-infected Merlot, Cabernet Franc and Cabernet Sauvignon, his aim is to make quite simply the best Bordeaux-style red blend in the country, concentrating on richness of fruit rather than over-extraction and over-wooding.

In signature style, this entrepreneurial winemaker has introduced a Cap Classique made from Shiraz, a local rarity pioneered in France and made popular in Australia. The intention is to funnel all or most of this variety into the sparkling wine. Meanwhile, lovers of Rhine Riesling will be happy to hear that he has planted a small vineyard of this classic German variety that has all but disappeared from the modern Cape wine scene. The first bottling reflects the light, floral Moselle style he intends to emulate.

After a morning or afternoon of tasting, enjoy a meal at Cassia, the contemporary restaurant at the entrance to the farm that offers eclectic food and sublime views from the sundeck.

details

🍷 **Wine tasting/sales:** Mon-Fri 9 am-5 pm; Sun 11 am-3 pm.
Closed Easter Friday and Sunday, 25 December and 1 January.

🛢 **Cellar tours:** by appointment.

🍽 **Restaurant:** Cassia, open for lunch Tues-Sun, dinner Tues-Sat;
tel. (+27-21) 976 0640.

💬 **Functions:** weddings, conferences and team-building events.

ⓘ **In addition:** Degustazione farmers' market on last Saturday of
each month.

☎ **Tel:** (+27-21) 976 1467.

🖱 **Website:** *www.nitida.co.za*

MEERENDAL

Durbanville

A trio of businessmen has turned historic
Meerendal into a delightful food and wine
destination, with the farm's own wines served
at three different restaurants.

Originally a wheat farm granted to Jan Meerland in 1702, Meerendal gained prominence as a wine farm in the course of the 20th century, under the ownership of the Starke family. It was William Starke who built the manor house in 1936, embellishing it with two distinctly different Cape Dutch gables, and his son 'Oom Kosie' who put Meerendal on the wine map in the 1970s, notably with Pinotage and Shiraz.

William's manor house, now restored, serves as the restaurant Wheatfields – one of only seven in the Cape winelands that have made it onto New York *Food & Wine*'s list of 'hottest' restaurants in the world – with the original farm title deeds and house plans displayed in a narrow passage behind the dining room. The passage windows overlook a sunny courtyard (where meals are sometimes served in summer) and beyond to vineyards reaching up the windswept slopes of the Dorstberg. These slopes have been identified as an ideal site for new plantings of Sauvignon Blanc and an exciting trial with tricky, cool-climate Pinot Noir. But the vineyards will extend only as far as the long-established cultivation line – the crown of the hill is being conserved for its rare renosterveld vegetation and the protection of a treasured small but growing herd of rhebok up in the kloof.

From the manor house's front *stoep*, the view that stretches across lawns, dams and fields to the distant Simonsberg and Helderberg mountains is the same that would have greeted 'Oom Kosie' each morning as he set off down to the cellar. Follow his footsteps down to The Cellar Door tasting room. A cosy place with wooden furniture and colourful kelims, this is where 'Oom Kosie' used to enjoy a glass of wine with his lunch.

When the new owners, a trio of behind-the-scenes businessmen, bought Meerendal in 2004, their plan was to develop the dilapidated family pile into a fine wine and food destination. And this they have done, but without losing the farm's links with the past. While ageing vineyards are being replanted, shy-bearing old stalwarts are nurtured to produce small quantities of exceptional wines. In the cellar, the original *kuipe* (open concrete fermentation tanks) are still in use for red wine, while stainless steel tanks and cooling equipment have been upgraded to improve the quality of the whites. All this has been achieved under the watchful eye of winemaker Liza Goodwin, whose 10-year tenure bridges the property's transformation. Bennie Howard, the veteran manager of the Nederburg Auction who was brought on board to manage Meerendal's metamorphosis, fondly recalls his annual visits to taste Meerendal's wines with 'Oom Kosie'.

A coterie of cooks turn out an eclectic range of dishes for Meerendal's three restaurants, each offering a very different dining experience. Elegant, award-winning Wheatfields serves lunches and dinners showcasing informed food-and-wine matches – a well-versed *sommelier* is on hand for guidance. Wines to match may include the trio in Meerendal's Prestige range: the delicately wooded Bin 242 Sauvignon Blanc (named after the farm's estate number); the award-winning Bin 159 Shiraz (reflecting the farm's title deed number); and the rich, spicy Heritage Block Pinotage, made from bush vines half-a-century old. Ideal with dessert will be a chilled thimbleful of honeyed Chenin Blanc Natural Sweet or the new Blanc de Blancs Cap Classique.

The Bistro provides casual fare in rainy-day comfort or on a breezy summer sundeck with sweeping views across Durbanville's farmlands. On wind-still days, tables and umbrellas are set out on a lawn big enough to host an impromptu soccer game.

Sunday is family day, when The Barn & Lawn throws open its doors, unfurls its umbrellas and sets its tables for a buffet lunch. This large, airy venue caters for any celebratory function, but many a bridal couple remember it as the perfect spot for a real farm wedding.

PREVIOUS SPREAD The coterie of cooks relish experimenting with food and wine at Meerendal's various eateries.

THIS SPREAD Traditional pasture and wheat lands have made way for vineyards.

Liza Goodwin has overseen the transformation of Meerendal's reds.

Fine dining at Wheatfields provides carefully selected wine and food pairings.

Restaurant staff are friendly and well versed.

Wheatfields is in the restored 1936 manor house with its replica of 17th-century Groot Constantia's Cape Dutch gable.

White ageing vineyards are being replanted, shy-bearing old stalwarts are nurtured to produce small quantities of exceptional wines

Don't miss... a walk to the wedding chapel with its traditional slave bell. This simple, beautiful building, with its pews of polished wood, has a lingering aroma of beeswax and straw from its days as a hay barn.

details

- **Wine tasting/sales:** daily 8 am-5 pm. Closed Easter Friday and 25 December. Tasting cost: R10 (refunded on purchase of 6 bottles).
- **Also for sale:** olives, preserves and other farm-style produce.
- **Restaurants:** Wheatfields, open Tues-Sat for lunch and dinner. The Bistro, open daily 8 am-5 pm for breakfast and lunch. The Barn & Lawn, open Sun from 12.30 pm for buffet lunch. Tel. (+27-21) 975 1655.
- **Functions:** chapel for wedding ceremonies. The Barn & Lawn and The Loft for wedding receptions, parties and conferences.
- (i) **In addition:** wheelchair friendly.
- **Children:** jungle gym, lawns.
- **Tel:** (+27-21) 975 1655.
- **Website:** *www.meerendal.co.za*

COLONA CASTLE

Lakeside, Cape Town

Located a short drive from Cape Town, Colona Castle is perched on the mountainside above Lakeside, overlooking Zandvlei and beyond to False Bay and distant Cape Hangklip, and across the Constantia winelands to Table Mountain and Devil's Peak. With so many attractions on its doorstep, it makes a quiet and relaxing base from which to explore Cape Town and the Cape Peninsula, the beautiful False Bay coast, and the wineries of Constantia and further afield.

Leisure activities in the area include mountain and beach walks, a range of watersports and whale watching in False Bay, birdwatching, and playing a round or two of golf at one of several world-class courses. Therapeutic massages and spa treatments can be arranged on request. The weather is pleasant all year, and generally warmer in winter and cooler in summer than surrounding areas.

The luxury boutique hotel's eight suites are elegantly furnished with treasured antiques and objets d'art collected over many years, yet provide all the modern comforts and amenities from under-floor heating to wireless internet and flat-screen satellite television. Personalised service ensures that guests feel welcome at all times, whether they're relaxing in the secluded haven of the mountain garden after a busy day's exploring, or unwinding in the outdoor swimming pool.

Dinner is our chef's skilful combination of the Cape's finest and freshest organic ingredients. Guests can enjoy it by candlelight in the superb architecture of the dining hall and, as they look out over city lights and moonlit sky, it makes a perfect end to the day.

details

How to get there
From Cape Town take the Van der Stel (M3) freeway to its end and turn right. Turn left into Stonehurst, keeping left at the circle and continue to the T-juncton with Boyes Drive. Turn right and drive for about 4 km to the left turn into Old Boyes Drive. At the sharp hairpin bend, turn left into Verwood Street.

Who to contact
Tel. (+27-21) 788 8235, e-mail *colona@link.co.za* or go to *www.colonacastle.co.za*

COLONA CASTLE (3)

THE CELLARS-HOHENORT

Constantia

The Constantia Valley was the first wine-producing area in the Cape, and it is fitting that one of the valley's early wine farms, Klaasenbosch, is now the core of one of the Cape's centres of hospitality: The Cellars-Hohenort. While the finely restored 18th-century Klaasenbosch wine cellars and the splendid Hohenort manor house represent the past, the rest of this elegant establishment is firmly ensconced in the present. Surrounded by four hectares of vineyards and beautifully landscaped gardens, this five-star Relais & Chateaux hotel boasts two fine restaurants, two more venues for intimate dining, and an aptly named bar – The Martini – which has a martini list second to none, as well as an extensive range of local wines.

The Greenhouse Restaurant is also well named, being built around a splendid old oak and having huge plate-glass windows that look onto eight ancient camphor trees in the tranquil garden. The Cape Malay Restaurant serves a wide range of authentic Cape Malay dishes – from *snoek* (fish) soup to *deningvleis* and *bobotie* (spicy meat dishes) – and is one of the few venues in Cape Town where this traditional local fare can be enjoyed.

Guests who want to work off the kilograms – or work up an appetite – can make use of one of the two swimming pools, the tennis court or the putting and chipping green, or they can explore the beautiful surroundings on a bicycle provided by the hotel. Alternatively, if pure relaxation is required, a visit to the Paris Spa will rejuvenate body and mind.

details

How to get there
From Cape Town follow the M3 (Edinburgh Drive) towards Muizenberg past the suburbs of Claremont, Bishopscourt and Wynberg and take Exit 14 to Constantia. Turn left at the intersection, drive under the bridge and at the second set of traffic lights turn right into Brommersvlei Road. Continue for 2.5 km to the hotel entrance on the left.

Who to contact
Tel. (+27-21) 794 2137, e-mail *cellars@relaischateaux.com* or go to *www.cellars-hohenort.com*

THE CELLARS-HOHENORT (4)

WHERE WINEMAKING

Stellenbosch North

Stellenbosch is arguably the wine capital of South Africa. Winemaking dates back to its settlement in the 17th century and remains the lifeblood of many of its people. To the visitor it offers a magnificent mix of history, natural beauty and warm hospitality. Its hills and mountains provide a variety of soils and micro-climates that make wine quality across the board a given. The northern reaches of the district are defined by the craggy Simonsberg mountain and its foothills: Simonsberg-Stellenbosch, Klapmutskop and Bottelary. Here you'll find historical Cape Dutch estates, old family farms and ultra-modern wineries, steeped in the tradition of winemaking and a newfound dedication to conservation and community upliftment.

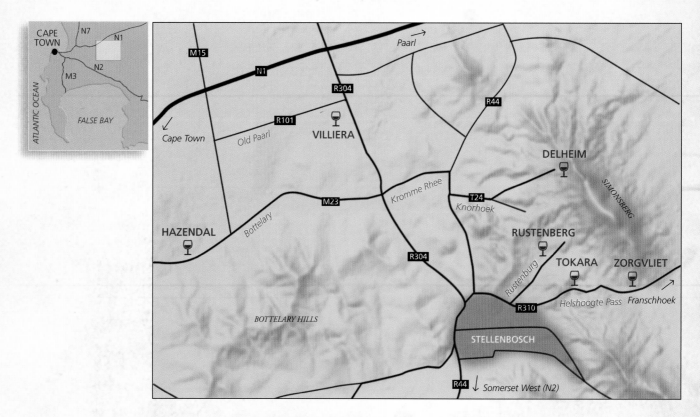

ROOTS RUN DEEP

HAZENDAL
Bottelary Hills

A Russian émigré imbued this old family wine farm

with eclectic charm, combining fine wine and food with

Cape Dutch history and Russian art and culture in a

thoroughly laid-back environment.

DEN 23 AUG
Aᵒ 1790

Where Cape Town's northern suburbs give way to the vineyards of Stellenbosch lies a wine farm that can only be described as eclectic.

White gateposts mark the start of a road that meanders through a reedbed of bulrushes and weeping willows and past the first hint of the farm's varied history: a 300-year-old livestock kraal with crumbling whitewashed walls and a tilting archway. Further on stands the 18th-century Cape Dutch manor house, with its distinctive baroque gable and solid oak door featuring an unusual filigree fanlight. The roof, originally thatched, was tiled some decades ago, an unusual feature that somehow adds to the farm's character.

Living quarters and a barn built in the early 1700s and converted into a cellar a hundred years later now serve as a tasting room, where sections of exposed masonry and a collection of prints, plaques and portraits provide a window into the past.

The property was granted to a German settler, Christoffel Haasenwinkel in 1704 and the classic H-shaped manor house was built in 1764 by a subsequent owner, Joost van As. His descendants finally sold to Izaak Bosman in 1831 and for the next 163 years Hazendal was home to five generations of Bosmans, whose history is depicted on a massive 'totem pole' topped with the bust of Oom Piet Bosman. He is credited with establishing the farm's reputation for fine wines – originally Chenin Blanc but later reds. Caught in Oom Piet's stern gaze is a portrait of the current owner, Russian émigré Mark Voloshin, who bought the struggling farm in 1994 and, with long-term partner Leo Schumacher, has breathed new life into it.

Born in Moscow where he studied dentistry, Voloshin's links to his Russian heritage have remained strong, as shown by the Marvol Museum of Russian Arts and Culture, tucked away in a

corner of the Hazendal cellar. It's a nostalgic collection of porcelain, samovars, exquisite wooden religious icons and traditionally painted Easter eggs. An upstairs gallery hung with Russian oils provides an eccentric setting for intimate wedding ceremonies.

Hazendal's sizable tasting area features leather sofas, a large central hearth with burnished copper flue, and a Bechstein, which is played as accompaniment to the lavish Sunday buffets in the adjoining Hermitage restaurant. A colourful ceiling mural depicting Hazendal's history provides an unusual backdrop to the dining experience, as do the plate-glass panels overlooking the stainless steel tanks and oak barrels in the modern cellar.

Red wines, particularly Cabernet Sauvignon and Shiraz, are the farm's forte, and it was a Shiraz/Cabernet blend that won for winemaker Ronell Wiid the prestigious annual Diners Club Winemaker of the Year Award in 1999 – the first time it went to a woman. Among the standard white classics, Chenin Blanc is another speciality, with an elegant, fruity wooded version produced from decades-old bush vines that were the source of well-loved Hazendal 'Steen' wines during the Bosman era. Wiid has also struck gold with an acclaimed dessert wine made from Chenin grapes. Its name, The Last Straw, is an allusion to the traditional French *vin de paille* method of drying fully ripe grapes on straw before allowing them to ferment into a rich wine with a typically apricot flavour. However, sparkling wine is Wiid's favourite tipple, so be sure to try her White Nights Brut Cap Classique.

Despite – or perhaps because of – its charming eclecticism, Hazendal has a delightfully laid-back ambience. A sunny summer's day calls for a leisurely lunch on the lawn, and there is plenty of room for an impromptu game of cricket or soccer – and plenty of bread crusts to feed to the geese and ducks on the farm dam.

Don't miss... the latest off-beat addition to Hazendal's repertoire: Die Plaasteater. A life-like glass-fibre cow marks the entrance to a local fringe music and cabaret venue next to a rambling old farm building. Enquire about complimentary tickets after an early dinner at The Hermitage.

PREVIOUS SPREAD The 18th-century manor house is a gracious backdrop for alfresco dining, picnics and lawn games.

THIS SPREAD Traditional Russian artefacts include intricately painted wooden eggs.

Hazendal's vines cover the Bottelary Hills opposite.

The satin-swagged Russian art gallery is a popular venue for intimate wedding ceremonies.

Red wines are the farm's forte.

The tasting room in an 18th-century building is a treasure trove of eclectic items.

details

- 🍷 **Wine tasting/sales:** Mon-Sun 9 am-4.30 pm. Closed Easter Friday, 25 December and 1 January. Tasting cost: R10 per 5 wines (refunded on purchase).
- 🛢 **Cellar tours:** for groups, by appointment.
- 🍽 **Restaurant:** The Hermitage, open 16 July-15 June, Tue-Sun 9 am-2.30 pm; also Wed/Thurs dinner by prior booking. Tel. (+27-21) 903 5112.
- **Functions:** weddings, conferences and seminars.
- 🏷 **Also for sale:** small selection of curios.
- 👫 **Children:** children's menu, jungle gym, lawns for ball games, feeding ducks on the dam.
- ⓘ **In addition:** Marvol Museum housing Russian art and artefacts. Local fringe theatre, cabaret and music in Die Plaasteater; tel. (+27-73) 869 1291 or (+27-72) 867 9555.
- ☎ **Tel:** (+27-21) 903 5112.
- 🖱 **Website:** www.hazendal.co.za

VILLIERA
Bottelary Hills

The Grier clan broke new ground on land with no

previous viticultural history, pioneering Cap Classique

production, keeping quality wines affordable and creating

their own tradition of easy, unpretentious hospitality.

Although best known for its pioneering Cap Classique sparkling wines, Villiera also produces serious Chenin Blancs, a classic red blend, some fine dessert specialities and a selection of palate- and pocket-friendly wines. This attractive farm is, moreover, home to the laid-back and friendly Grier clan.

Jeff, quietly passionate about wine, is the winemaker and his cousin Simon is the farm manager, viticulturist and conservationist. On the business side, Jeff's sister Cathy, a graduate of the Prue Leith cookery school in London, looks after marketing, sales and exports while her husband, Englishman Julian Brewer, has been roped in for the 'invaluable but unenviable' role of logistics manager for an enterprise that moves nearly 130 000 cases of wine around the world annually (including special bottlings for Woolworths in South Africa and Marks & Spencer in Britain). All four are involved in community projects: advising a neighbouring emerging wine farmer, providing infrastructure for after-school facilities for farm workers' children, and donating land and expertise for an agricultural endeavour by nearby township dwellers.

You may find yourself chatting to any one of the Griers during your visit. Draw them out, for they'll be characteristically modest about their achievement in transforming what was an inauspicious flatland farm between Stellenbosch and Paarl in 1983 into a top wine property. The terroir is not conventionally superior in viticultural terms, but low fertility from mostly sandy and clay, gravel soils results in naturally small yields that benefit fruit intensity – and helped Jeff realise his dream of making sparkling wine *à la Champagne*, with the encouragement of Jean-Louis Denois, a Champenoise who has since become a family friend.

In the 1980s, Jeff was one of the pioneers in establishing guidelines for the local production and quality of authentically bottle-fermented sparkling wine. This led to the officially sanctioned designation 'Cap Classique' for South Africa's leading sparkling wines, which international law prohibited from being called Champagne, even though traditional *champenoise* methods were used to produce them.

The various stages in the production of Cap Classique can be followed in Villiera's large cellar that dates from the mid-20th century. Original concrete and fibreglass tanks squat alongside the latest in stainless steel, and a wooden 'skywalk' takes you into the hub of the production cellar. From there you can watch the push-button gyropalette that has replaced the laborious traditional manual riddling process and, through the window onto the disgorging line, catch the excitement of *dégorgement*.

Besides the Tradition Brut NV and Brut Rosé NV (which has the novel addition of Pinotage), Villiera makes the Monro Brut, a classic Chardonnay/Pinot Noir blend that, disgorged after five years on the lees, is a particularly special cuvée. Champagne devotees frustrated by allergies should look out for the Brut Natural, a pure Chardonnay, bone-dry Cap Classique made only with yeast found naturally on the grape skin.

Doing things nature's way is integral to the Griers' philosophy of wine growing. Besides tending Villiera's 260 hectares of vineyard planted to some 13 different varieties, viticulturist Simon is an avid conservator. A large tract of farmland has been restored to indigenous vegetation, encouraging the return of wildlife, and the proliferation of small buck species induced him to collaborate with a game expert on a fenced-off haven for larger buck. Ducks and guineafowl do the work of chemical pesticides, and Simon has even provided nesting boxes for the resident Cape eagle-owls that may be seen in the massive oaks outside the tasting room – or happily roosting outside the boxes!

After tasting the wines and exploring the cellar, make yourself at home on the oak-shaded patio with whatever provisions you've brought along (feel free to ask for crockery and cutlery) or relax on the grass under a giant fig tree next to the vines.

PREVIOUS SPREAD Eco-friendly farming has brought wildlife, like this steenbok doe, back into the vineyards.

Villiera's flatland with the Simonsberg peak on the horizon.

THIS SPREAD Looking out from the cellar.

Ladybirds keep vine pests like mealy bug at bay.

Villiera's sparkling wine inspired a jeweller's creativity.

Vintner Jeff Grier checks a Brut Rosé riddled by gyropalette.

A farm crèche among the vines.

Don't miss... tasting the Domaine Grier wines, made on the family's Roussillon property near Perpignan in the south of France. This 22-hectare vineyard specialises in red varieties such as Shiraz, Grenache and Carignan, from which Jeff is producing wines full of fruit and spice.

Jeff was one of the pioneers in establishing guidelines for the local production of bottle-fermented sparkling wine

details

🍷 **Wine tasting/sales:** Mon-Fri 8.30 am-5 pm; Sat 8.30 am-3 pm. Closed Easter Friday and Sunday, 25 December and 1 January. Tasting cost: no charge.

🛢 **Cellar tour:** self-guided during tasting hours; guided by appointment.

🧺 **Picnics:** BYO in summer.

🏷 **Also for sale:** half-barrels for sale when available.

👫 **Children:** welcome, but no special provision made.

ⓘ **In addition:** annual St Vincent's Harvest Day celebration on Saturday closest to 22 January (proceeds to charities such as Pebbles education project for farm children); booking required. Visits to game sanctuary, by appointment.

☎ **Tel:** (+27-21) 865 2002/3.

🖱 **Website:** *www.villiera.com*

DELHEIM
Simonsberg

The home of three generations of Sperlings, this farm
deep in a Simonsberg kloof is the birthplace of good,
old-fashioned Cape winelands hospitality, where wine,
food and good company have long been enjoyed.

On 19 April 1951 Michael Sperling, a 20-year-old German of aristocratic descent, disembarked in Table Bay harbour with little more than a suitcase, change from a £10 note and no knowledge of any of the local languages. He had come to the Cape to start a new life on a farm called Driesprong, the home of his mother's cousin Del and her husband Hans Hoheisen.

More than half a century later, 'Spatz' (sparrow) Sperling is hailed as a pioneer of the 20th-century Cape wine industry and a driving force behind the first wine route, the first public wine auction and a now-flourishing local food and wine culture. Although the Sperling family has only recently taken over full ownership of Delheim, the farm has to all intents and purposes been its home – and passion – for more than 50 years. Patriarchal Spatz and his Dutch-born wife Vera now leave the day-to-day running of the farm to two of their four children: Victor manages the vineyards and cellar (assisted by winemaker Brenda van Niekerk) and Nora handles marketing, sales and exports.

The close-knit family live in various homes around the winery, all linked by bricked pathways and shaded by massive oak, yellow-wood and plane trees. You could bump into any one of them going about their work during the week, probably with a young Sperling and a few Jack Russells in tow.

A guided tour of the cellar is recommended for newcomers to wine. While learning about the technicalities of making wine, you'll hear some entertaining anecdotes about life on this characterful wine farm. There was the time when young Spatz, overcome by fumes from a tank of fermenting wine, toppled off a ladder. Or when Katy the cow licked up some leaking Pinotage, collapsed in a drunken stupor and, despite all efforts at resuscitation, finally expired. Or when, in the 1960s, a critical German friend tasted Spatz's first attempt at a sweet Late Harvest wine and pronounced it 'Dreck' (rubbish). The irreverent Spatz coined the name Spatzendreck (sparrow droppings) for the wine.

Delheim's wines today are anything but Dreck. They come from the original Driesprong farm's vineyards behind the winery and from excellent viticultural land just across the R44. Bought in the 1970s and '80s and now amalgamated under the name Delvera, this is the source of some of Delheim's finest Cabernet Sauvignon, Merlot and Shiraz for the acclaimed Grand Reserve Bordeaux-style blend and single-vineyard Vera Cruz Shiraz. The farm's Chardonnays are particularly good too, notably the barrel-fermented Sur Lie, and dessert wine connoisseurs should try the Natural Sweet and the award-winning Edelspatz Noble Late Harvest.

The farm has traditionally produced wines for a wide range of tastes, including its enduring Pinotage Rosé and a semi-sweet Gewürztraminer, a variety that is seldom vinified nowadays but recalls the strong German influence on Delheim. That influence is also seen in the tasting room, a cosy red-brick alcove reminiscent of a Weinstube. The restaurant menu reflects it too, with German specialities such as Bratwurst and Leberwurst alongside traditional South African fare like snoek (fish), springbok and lamb shank.

Delheim has long been a member of the BWI (Biodivesity & Wine Initiative) and recently earned championship status with Victor's groundbreaking cellar waste-water management scheme that involves a natural water clarification system, including final filtration through an indigenous wetland area. The Sperlings have also played a leading role in establishing the Klapmutskop Renosterveld Conservancy, based around Klapmutskop on Delvera. Three different geological formations meet here and support rare indigenous fynbos vegetation, as well as a centuries-old yellowwood forest recently discovered during a major clearing of alien plants.

Don't miss... a full-moon guided hike up Klapmutskop followed by a stay at Oakleaf Lodge on Delvera, where walks start and finish. A farmhouse renovated by Victor's wife Ronél, Oakleaf is set in lush gardens with a swimming pool.

The Sperlings have also played a leading role in establishing the Klapmutskop Renosterveld Conservancy

PREVIOUS SPREAD Dormant vines on the Simonsberg slopes.

THIS SPREAD The cosy tasting room is reminiscent of a German *Weinstube*.

'Spatz' and Vera Sperling often hike up to the family's private graveyard near the 17th-century ruins of the home of the local gunner whose cannon signalled the arrival of ships in Table Bay.

Table Mountain and Lion's Head from the car park.

The vintner and his Jack Russell on a cellar wall mural.

A Cape classic quaffing wine and international bestseller, ideal with light lunches.

details

- 🍷 **Wine tasting/sales:** Mon-Sun 9 am-5 pm. Closed Easter Friday and Sunday, 25 December and 1 January. Tasting cost: R20; R25 including cellar tour.
- 🛢 **Cellar tours:** Mon-Sun 10.30 am and 2.30 pm.
- 🍽 **Restaurant:** Garden Restaurant, open daily 9.30 am-4.30 pm. Tel. (+27-21) 888 4607.
- 🏠 **Accommodation:** Oakleaf Lodge on Delheim's sister farm Delvera offers rooms and a separate honeymoon suite in a self-catering farmhouse. Tel. (+27-82) 809 9878 or (+27-21) 884 4079.
- 🏷 **Also for sale:** curios, clothing, produce, wine books.
- 👪 **Children:** welcome, but no special provision made.
- ⓘ **In addition:** exhibition vineyard showing grape varieties; riverside picnic area; vineyard walks; mountain bike trails through Klapmutskop Renosterveld Conservancy on Delvera – contact Dirtopia on (+27-21) 884 4752.
- ☎ **Tel:** (+27-21) 888 4600.
- 🖱 **Website:** *www.delheim.com*

RUSTENBERG

Simonsberg

One of the Cape's most venerable farms continues to make world-famous wines, while sensitive restoration of its historic homesteads and beautiful gardens continues under the loving custodianship of the Barlow family.

Rustenberg's self-described 'custodian' has overseen the evolution of this wine farm from a venerable Cape First Growth to a 21st-century South African benchmark on the international stage

Don't miss... walking the Chartres Labyrinth in solitude. Based on the floor design of 12th-century Chartres Cathedral, its 34 loops are laid out on a lawn in brick and cobblestone and end in a six-petalled grass rose representing the six kingdoms to be visited in search of spiritual enlightenment: plant, mineral, animal, human, angelic and the unknown.

PREVIOUS SPREAD Private guests staying at historic Cape Dutch jewel Schoongezicht follow in the footsteps of Rudyard Kipling, George Bernard Shaw and Scott of the Antarctic.

THIS SPREAD Vines beneath the Simonsberg peak.

The stylish yet informal tasting area that extends into a cosy lounge and patio.

Spring flowers in Rozanne Barlow's formal English country garden.

The garden's summerhouse.

An offspring of the farm's champion Jersey bull whose name lives on in the Brampton range of quality quaffers.

The Barlows of Rustenberg are descended from an old Lancashire family dating back to the rule of Richard II. So it is perhaps not surprising that William Shakespeare's *King Richard II* may drift into your thoughts as you approach the winery through a gentle landscape of green trees and pastures dotted with soft-eyed Jersey cows: 'This happy breed of men, this little world … this blessed plot, this earth, this realm, this England.' But then the imposing Simonsberg rearing up behind a vintage Cape Dutch farmhouse brings you back to the Stellenbosch winelands with a bump.

Rustenberg's history, dating back to the late 17th century, is steeped in not only English tradition, but also the Cape Dutch influences on wine farming and architecture in South Africa. The limited-edition book on Rustenberg, regularly updated and usually available from the tasting room, will tell you more, and there is no better way to spend a winter's day than beside the log fire with a glass of Peter Barlow or John X Merriman at your elbow and the book on your knee. Although minimalist in design, with spiral stairs leading down into a space that combines steel and glass with slate, wood and raw brick, the tasting room has a convivial air.

Simon Barlow took over the reins at Rustenberg in 1987 from his late mother Pam, who had been managing vineyards, cellar, orchards and dairy since the death of her husband Peter in 1975. They had re-united Rustenberg (the private family home) and Schoongezicht (the hub of farming activity, including the wine cellar and tasting room) in the 1960s, restoring both historic homesteads. According to architectural historians Hans Fransen and Mary Cook, Schoongezicht 'has few equals in the Cape and its front façade is in perfect order'.

Simon, trained in agriculture and a progressive thinker (he's a former governor of the Agriculture, Food and Industry Section of the World Economic Forum which meets in Davos, Switzerland, each year), is committed to farm community upliftment and environmental conservation projects. Farm workers run a trout-breeding scheme on farm dams. As a BWI (Biodiversity & Wine Initiative) member, Rustenberg focuses on eradicating alien vegetation and protecting wetland, costly exercises for a 1200-hectare private spread.

Most importantly, Rustenberg's self-described 'custodian' has overseen the evolution of this wine farm from a venerable Cape First Growth to a 21st-century South African benchmark on the international stage. In the vineyards he has developed new clones, planted experimental varieties as components to enrich award-winning blends, installed futuristic water management and measuring systems, and set up a private nursery to ensure virus-free plant material. In the 1990s, a multi-million overhaul of the Schoongezicht homestead included cleverly incorporating hi-tech tank, barrel and bottling facilities in historic farm buildings. In these peaceful surroundings, it's not easy to imagine beneath your feet a tunnel along which wine, barrels and winemaker Randolph Christians (a farm veteran) and his workers move between the semi-subterranean fermentation cellar, the underground barrel maturation room and the bottling line in the original 18th-century cellar.

Reds are Rustenberg's forte, and they include the Peter Barlow, a rare Cabernet Sauvignon from a single vineyard of 20-year-old vines; the John X Merriman, one of the Cape's finest Bordeaux-style blends whose name recalls a former owner of Schoongezicht and prime minister of the Cape in the early 20th century; and an exciting newcomer in the form of a Shiraz (labelled Syrah). Among the whites, Chardonnays demonstrate the versatility of this grape. The rich Five Soldiers comes from a single vineyard where five tall pine trees stand guard, while the Stellenbosch Chardonnay emphasises regionality and the third wine is unoaked.

details

🍷 **Wine tasting/sales:** Mon-Fri 9 am-4.30 pm; Sat 10 am-1.30 pm; public holidays 9 am-4 pm. Closed Easter Friday, 25 December and 1 January. Tasting cost: no charge.

🧍 **Children:** welcome, but no special provision made.

ℹ️ **In addition:** free access to the English country garden and the labyrinth.

☎ **Tel:** (+27-21) 809 1200.

🖱 **Website:** *www.rustenberg.co.za*

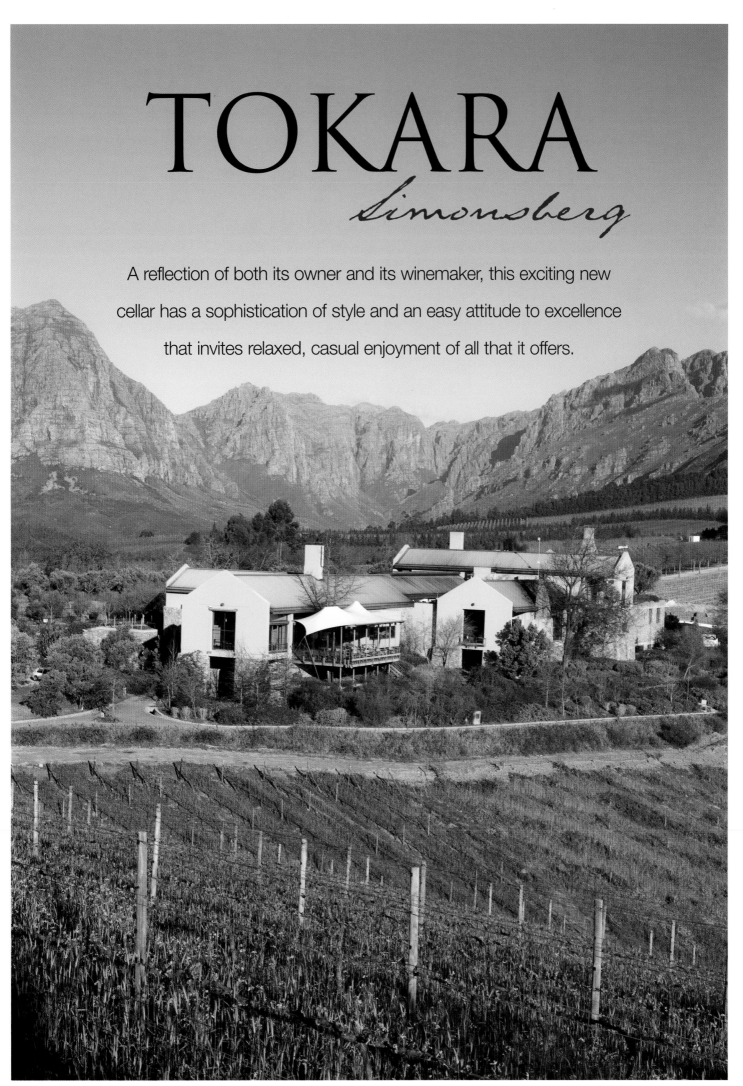

TOKARA

Simonsberg

A reflection of both its owner and its winemaker, this exciting new

cellar has a sophistication of style and an easy attitude to excellence

that invites relaxed, casual enjoyment of all that it offers.

Banker GT Ferreira bought the farm Rust en Vrede on the crest of the Helshoogte Pass in 1994 as a family home with fabulous views. While still a student at Stellenbosch University he had developed a love of wine, so it wasn't too difficult for renowned Thelema vintner Gyles Webb to persuade his new neighbour to make the most of the area's excellent viticultural potential and get into wine farming. The giant puzzle piece mounted at the winery entrance signifies Tokara's subsequent mercurial rise, identifying it as a member of the stellar wine ward of Simonsberg, a bench of farms producing premium wine (mainly red) on the mountain's south-facing slopes. Each of the other farms displays another piece of the puzzle.

With Webb's help, Ferreira planted classic wine varieties on the various slopes of the hilly landscape. He also built a new hi-tech cellar, making Tokara winery into an architect's vision in stone, glass and steel. Wooden decks offer breathtaking views across the Stellenbosch winelands to Table Mountain and on a clear day you can see False Bay, source of the summer Southeaster. Together with altitude – the surrounding vineyards are more than 400 metres

above sea level – this cool wind provides the low temperatures that contribute to the excellence of Tokara's wines.

Miles Mossop, one of a new generation of talented Cape winemakers, came on board in 2000 to launch the first wines from still-youthful vines under the Zondernaam label – a reference to the property's original 17th-century listing as 'the farm with no name'. This became the farm's second label when Tokara, an amalgamation of the names of Ferreira's son Thomas and daughter Kara, was introduced in 2005. Tokara is reserved for the farm's premium wines: a Bordeaux-style red blend, a white blend, a Stellenbosch Chardonnay and a Walker Bay Sauvignon Blanc. By then Ferreira's holding of more than 100 hectares included two vineyards in the prime cool-climate areas of Elgin and the Hemel-en-Aarde Valley. The two labels also denote an overall difference in style: Tokara recalls the Old World in the European tradition of making wines with longevity by combining power and elegance, fruit and structure, whereas Zondernaam caters for New World tastes for wines that are full-fruited and more gently wooded, with easy charm and accessibility.

Having admired the vistas through the picture windows on one side of Tokara's tasting room, walk across for a bird's-eye view into the fermentation cellar. To get a peek into the dimly lit barrel maturation cellar, descend the steel staircase from the restaurant deck into the garden created by Ferreira's wife Anne-Marie and follow a gravel pathway between Cape honeysuckle and rambling roses to the viewing window. The olive groves that have become a feature of the farm and cellar landscape are another of Anne-Marie's projects. She manages the Olive Shed over the hill, home of Tokara's award-winning single-varietal and premium extra virgin olive oils.

Recalling how, as a student in straitened circumstances, he was grateful when tastings on wine farms were free, Ferreira doesn't charge for wine tastings but welcomes all. 'They're the wine lovers and buyers of the future,' he maintains. That is also why Tokara's tasting room is one of the few that are open on Saturdays, Sundays and public holidays – and why you can either perch sociably at the long counter and talk wine to the well-informed young pourers, or retreat with your glass to a comfortable armchair in front of the open hearth.

Next door, Cape chef Etienne Bonthuys and his team entertain in an open-plan kitchen. Officially termed 'contemporary classic', his creative cooking is renowned for its tendency to surprise. All Tokara's wines feature on the wine list, so you may want to start there and select dishes to suit.

PREVIOUS SPREAD Veteran Cape chef Etienne Bonthuys makes the most of Tokara's award-winning wines and olive oils.

Tokara blends cement, steel and stone with open-plan interiors, windows and decks for wonderful views.

THIS SPREAD Anne-Marie Ferreira's Olive Shed produces rare single-varietal olive oils from Mission, Frantoio and Leccino olives, and a blend with Coratina.

'Plum pudding hill' with its contoured vineyards and olive grove.

Tokara lies on a foothill of the Simonsberg.

Look down from the mezzanine tasting area into the hi-tech cellar.

The open-plan tasting area includes an art gallery and pieces from the owner's private collection.

Don't miss... sipping a snifter of Tokara's five-year-old pot-still brandy made in traditional Cognac style. Quantities are minute, so it's worth every cent of the small fee. Try it with a slim slab of exotic pink peppercorn or orange-flavoured imported dark chocolate specially wrapped for the tasting room.

details

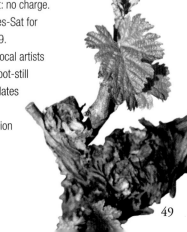

🍷 **Wine tasting/sales:** Mon-Fri 9 am-5 pm; Sat/Sun and public holidays 10 am-3 pm. Tasting cost: no charge.

🍽 **Restaurant:** Tokara Restaurant, open Tues-Sat for lunch and dinner. Tel. (+27-21) 808 5959.

🏷 **Also for sale:** works by up-and-coming local artists at Art @ Tokara in the foyer; farm's own pot-still brandy, olives and olive oils, exotic chocolates in the tasting room.

👪 **Children:** welcome, but no special provision made.

☎ **Tel:** (+27-21) 808 5900.

🖱 **Website:** *www.tokara.com*

ZORGVLIET

Banhoek

This idyllic wine farm in a valley between two mountain peaks invites

a prolonged stay with delights for body and soul, from great wine

and food to vigorous vineyard walks and soothing spa treatments.

As you crest the Helshoogte Pass that links Stellenbosch and Franschhoek, you're greeted by one of the most spectacular views in the Cape winelands: the green Banhoek Valley between the crags of the Simonsberg and the Klein Drakenstein Mountains. In late October, as you're driving to Zorgvliet wine farm, lodge and spa, you'll see budding vines, orchards in blossom and white-fenced horse paddocks.

Plan your visit around a pre-booked cellar tour with young winemaker Neil Moorhouse, whose enthusiasm and knowledge of the inner workings of his ultra-sophisticated cellar know no bounds. He'll talk gravity feed, conveyor-belt systems, custom-built tanks, automated punch-downs and computerised cooling systems. Then he'll show you his I-Phone, which automatically alerts him to the smallest change or slightest glitch in the wine-making process and allows him to key in new settings and adjustments via a computerised monitoring system – even when he's on a marketing trip in London!

On the road side of the cellar is the 'Golden Mile', comprising blocks of classic red varieties that go into the farm's flagship Bordeaux-style red blend, Richelle (named after owner Mac van der Merwe's granddaughter). A Cabernet Sauvignon and a Sauvignon Blanc complete the trio of premium Zorgvliet wines. In addition, the farm's extensive Silver Myn range covers most varieties: look out for the Viognier, the Sémillon and the new Pinot Noir, as well as the Petit Verdot, a gorgeous red made from a variety seldom bottled on its own.

You can get a closer look at the Golden Mile and the high-lying vineyards on a walk conducted by a 'vine ranger', one of the vineyard workers schooled as guides by viticulturist Rudolf Jansen van Vuuren. And, if you ask Auburn, the young tasting room attendant,

Dinner guests can enjoy a flute of sparkling wine as they watch the surrounding mountains turn pink in the sunset

Don't miss... being pampered at the Zorgvliet Spa. Day visitors or overnight guests can try local spa products made from grape extracts: Sauvignon Blanc shampoo, Pinotage bath treatment or Cabernet body lotion.

PREVIOUS SPREAD Alfresco dining on the lodge's patio.

A view from Zorgvliet Lodge, overlooking the 'Golden Mile' of classic red varieties running down to the tasting room and cellar.

THIS SPREAD Premium red grapes destined for the Richelle flagship blend.

A late-afternoon back massage at the lake-side spa.

The new, ultra-modern cellar with vineyards climbing the Simonsberg behind.

Zorgvliet winemaker Neil Moorhouse monitoring barrel-maturing reds.

The centuries-old original wine cellar is now a wedding chapel.

you can learn about the Silver Myn label, which recalls an 18th-century conman and his search for silver in these mountains.

If it's lunch time, cross the stream below the cellar and walk down to Zorgvliet's hidden gem: a picnic area in a sunlit, wind-free dell in a wood. One end is family friendly, with tables, umbrellas, braai spots, a jungle gym and a jumping castle; the other is quieter and you can spread a blanket, open a bottle of chilled wine and snack from a substantial picnic basket provided by the deli and coffee shop.

Alternatively, breakfast, lunch or dine at the Herenhuis restaurant, located in the restored late 17th-century Cape Dutch manor house. Meals are served in several intimate dining rooms and the cuisine is contemporary South African, with the likes of venison, braised oxtail, *bobotie* (a Cape Malay curried mince dish) and malva pudding (a saucy baked dessert) on the menu. Each dish comes with a Zorgvliet wine recommendation. Dinner guests who arrive early can enjoy a flute of sparkling wine on the front *stoep* as they watch the surrounding mountains turn pink in the sunset.

Behind the Herenhuis, the centuries-old wine cellar is now a chapel, with stained-glass windows, wooden pews and chandeliers softly lighting the high-beamed thatched ceiling. Post-ceremony canapés and wine can be enjoyed in a stylishly converted farm building nearby, with its large verandah and cosy indoor hearth. Small conferences are held here too, while more intimate executive meetings and seminars take place next door in the Petit Verdot Room.

An overnight stay at the Vineyard Lodge & Spa completes the Zorgvliet experience. Fountains playing in the gravel courtyard create a sense of timelessness, while the high-ceilinged interiors, with dark wood furniture and autumn-hued curtaining, recall an era of elegance. The dining room opens onto a terrace, where supper under the stars is recommended in summer. On cool winter evenings, guests can adjourn to the cosy lounge for soup and freshly baked bread. And from every window there is that unforgettable view of the Banhoek Valley and the surrounding mountains.

details

🍷 **Wine tasting/sales:** Nov and Feb-April, Mon-Thurs 9 am-5 pm, Fri 9 am-6 pm, Sat 10 am-7 pm, Sun 10 am-5 pm; May-Oct, Mon-Fri 9 am-5 pm, Sat/Sun 11 am-5 pm; Dec/Jan and public holidays daily 10 am-3 pm. Closed Easter Friday and 25 December. Tel. (+27-21) 885 2547. Tasting cost: R15.

🛢 **Cellar/vineyard tours:** by appointment; tel. (+27-21) 885 1049.

🍽 **Restaurants:** Herenhuis, open daily 8 am-9.30 pm; tel. (+27-21) 885 2580. Zorgvliet coffee shop/deli/picnics, open Wed-Sun 9 am-6 pm; tel. (+27-82) 959 8619.

💼 **Functions:** weddings, seminars and conferences; tel. (+27-21) 885 1399.

🏠 **Accommodation:** *****Zorgvliet Vineyard Lodge, with pool; tel. (+27-21) 885 1791.

👪 **Children:** jungle gym and jumping castle at the picnic site; jungle gym at the Herenhuis restaurant.

ⓘ **In addition:** Zorgvliet Spa, with three overnight suites and a pool; tel. (+27-21) 885 2483.

🖱 **Website:** *www.zorgvliet.com*

JOURNEY OF
Stellenbosch South

This part of the Stellenbosch winelands is dominated by the Stellenbosch and Helderberg mountains and, further south, by the magnificent Hottentots Holland range. Enclaves like Papegaaiberg and Stellenboschkloof, as well as the Helderberg bench, are prime red wine country, although high-lying vineyards, with views across to False Bay in the cold Atlantic Ocean, also produce outstanding Sauvignon Blancs. But varied aspects ensure you'll find great wines in all styles here, attracting some of the Cape's top winemakers. On many of these farms, wines go hand in hand with food, whether it be award-winning restaurant fare, a sophisticated forest picnic or a fascinating sensory experience with wine and chocolate.

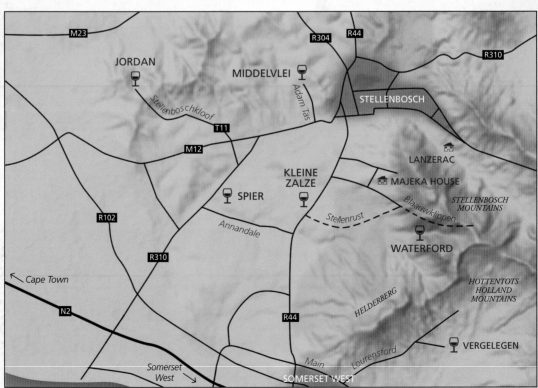

THE SENSES

SPIER

Stellenbosch

The scope of activities here may overwhelm. But a closer look

reveals remarkable places and experiences for a great family

getaway. And wine lovers won't be disappointed either...

An early start is highly recommended for a visit to this Mecca of entertainment that includes wine tastings, picnics, a choice of restaurants, horse riding and close encounters with cheetahs and birds of prey. Your first stop is likely to be at the Welcome Winetasting Centre, right next to the parking area, if only to pick up a map of Spier to help you find your way around. But linger for a while to taste some of the farm's everyday wines and, during harvest, samples of whichever grape varieties have been picked in the cool dawn hours in the vineyards across the Eerste River.

If you're a serious wine lover, though, continue straight to the Wine Centre, situated in one of the farm's few remaining original Cape Dutch buildings, where you'll find Spier Wines' extremely knowledgeable stalwarts, Francois van der Walt and Nikki Smit. Tastings are offered in all kinds of permutations that showcase Spier's various ranges of increasingly acclaimed wines made by Frans Smit. One tasting, for example, pairs any three single-varietal wines with different specially selected farm cheeses, allowing you to explore the interaction between flavours; another matches three premium wines with fresh samples of the typical aromas found on each, such as black pepper, coffee or vanilla sugar. And if you're visiting from a European Union country, you can log in your order and have the wine delivered to your home within 48 hours.

At Spier you can meet 10 captive-bred cheetahs and also learn about the recent introduction of Anatolian Shepherd dogs to protect livestock in southern Africa

Don't miss... walking beyond moyo to see restoration work being done on the original Cape Dutch manor house, once the home of the Joubert family from whom entrepreneur Dick Enthoven bought Spier in 1993. In the 1970s, the late Niel Joubert was one of the founding members of the Stellenbosch Wine Route, the forerunner of modern Cape winelands tourism. The farm's original deed of sale, dated 1692, still hangs in the manor house.

PREVIOUS SPREAD Traditional African musicians entertain at moyo restaurant.

Picnic beside the tranquil dam.

THIS SPREAD Casual tastings at the Welcome Winetasting Centre.

Spier's vineyards across the Eerste River, backed by the Helderberg.

moyo combines feasts and fairytales.

Cheetah Outreach volunteer handler Kate Booker introduces Hemingway.

Afro-chic in the Spier Hotel foyer.

Although winemaking is still a major activity at Spier – as it has been for nearly three centuries – today a lot more is going on too. Cheetahs, for example, roam in five hectares of grassed camps, the focus of an independently run educational and conservation support programme working in tandem with the CITES-registered De Wildt breeding centre and cheetah research in Namibia and Botswana. Cheetah Outreach was started here in 1997 to raise awareness, particularly in schools and the farming community, of the falling numbers of free-ranging cheetahs as a result of shrinking habitat and hunting by farmers in a misguided attempt to protect their livestock. Over the past century the cheetah population worldwide has declined from about 100 000 to 10 000, of which fewer than 1000 live in South Africa. At Spier you can meet 10 captive-bred cheetahs and also learn about the recent introduction of Anatolian Shepherd dogs to protect livestock in southern Africa, as they have done traditionally in their Turkish homeland.

Next door is Eagle Encounters, an open-air bird-of-prey centre where close encounters with rehabilitated indigenous eagles, falcons, hawks and owls enable you to appreciate the majesty of these magnificent birds.

Whatever you may fancy for lunch, you'll find it at Spier. Pre-order a picnic basket or put one together from the deli next to the Wine Centre, then pick the perfect spot on lawns, beneath trees and amid massive granite boulders surrounding a tranquil dam. Fish and flocks of geese and ducks will be waiting for your titbits. The Deck Restaurant overlooking the dam (no booking required) is an alternative – an Egyptian goose and her latest brood, including the occasional adopted white duck, often follow visitors there. Further down the banks of the Eerste River, the indoor/outdoor Jonkershuis Restaurant specialises in Cape country buffets. Then there's moyo, a sprawling Moroccan tent town with tree-house tables, ladders and staircases, cascading water streams, ethnic face-painting and 'jungle' scenes straight out of JM Barrie's *Peter Pan*, as well as a mouth-watering buffet catering for some 1500 diners.

details

🍷 **Wine tasting/sales:** Spier Welcome Centre tasting 10 am-4.30 pm daily; tasting costs Standard – R10, with cheese platter – R60; tel. (+27-21) 809 1157. Spier Wine Centre tasting 10 am-4.30 pm daily; tasting costs Standard – R10, Educational – R20, Sensory – R35, other options available; sales 9 am-5 pm daily; tel. (+27-21) 809 1143/6.

🏷 **Also for sale:** deli products, including wine-filled chocolates at Welcome Centre. Curios at Spier Gift Shop and Craft Market.

🍽 **Restaurants:** Jonkershuis for Cape country buffet; tel. (+27-21) 809 1159/72. moyo for lunch and dinner buffet; tel. (+27-21) 809 1133. Spier Hotel Restaurant for breakfast and dinner, and Wine Bar for light lunch; tel. (+27-21) 809 1100. Spier Deli for picnics; tel. (+27-21) 809 1152/3.

🎤 **Functions:** conferences and meetings in the Conference Centre and The Bomas respectively; tel. (+27-21) 809 1100. moyo for functions and weddings; tel. (+27-21) 809 1133.

🏠 **Accommodation:** ****Spier Hotel, village style setting; tel. (+27-21) 809 1100.

👫 **Children:** fully catered for.

ℹ️ **In addition:** Cheetah Outreach; tel. (+27-21) 881 3242. Eagle Encounters; tel. (+27-21) 858 1826. Horse riding; tel. (+27-21) 881 3683. Beam Gallery; tel. (+27-21) 809 1100. Camelot Spa at Spier; tel. (+27-21) 809 1931.

🖱 **Website:** *www.spier.co.za*

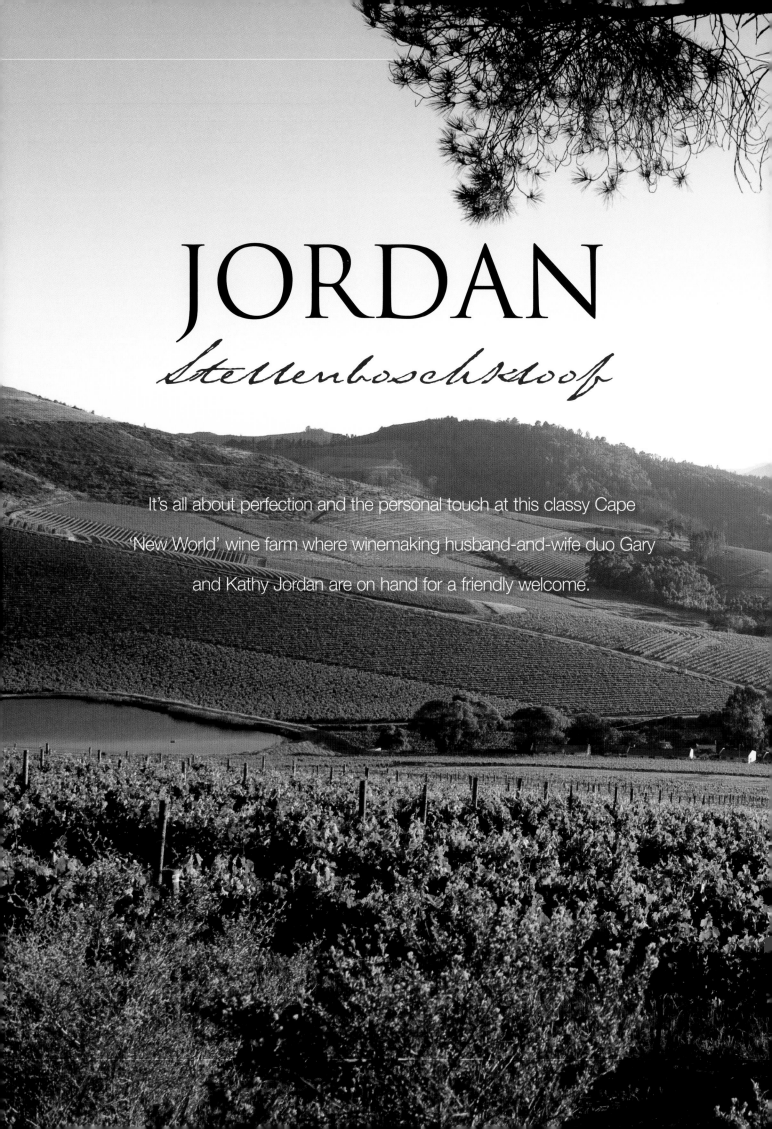

JORDAN

Stellenboschkloof

It's all about perfection and the personal touch at this classy Cape 'New World' wine farm where winemaking husband-and-wife duo Gary and Kathy Jordan are on hand for a friendly welcome.

The farm relies solely on water from two natural springs and its dams are rich in birdlife — the evocative call of the fish eagle is often heard

This family winery epitomises South Africa as a 'New World' wine country, which is not surprising, given the credentials and experience of husband-and-wife duo Gary and Kathy Jordan. He's a geologist, she's an economist and they studied winemaking at the University of California, Davis, during a two-year stint in the United States. They brought all their new skills to bear when they built the Jordan winery in 1992 and continued developing the vineyards that Gary's father Ted had started replanting a decade before.

Situated at the top of Stellenboschkloof, Jordan is the last stop on a narrow road that dissects the small valley. You can book a tour of the vineyards and cellar, and either Gary or Kathy will lead it if they are available. But even if they're busy pruning vines or overseeing the racking of a batch of wine, they'll make a point of joining you at some stage.

The tour starts on a grassy hill where – with a glass of chilled Sauvignon Blanc in hand – you look out over a patchwork of mountain-fringed vineyards. Just over 100 of the farm's 146 hectares are planted with vines, on various different soils and on slopes facing north, south, east and west. Such diversity of both aspect and soil is rare, and underpins Jordan's outstanding quality across a wide range of wines.

Altitudes on the farm vary too, from 165 to more than 400 metres, and the next stop is at a higher point, from which there are views of distant False Bay, Table Mountain and Table Bay. Here you'll get right in among the vines for a look at buds, berries and leaves, and your guide will point out the 20-year-old vineyard that produces Jordan's acclaimed Nine Yards Chardonnay. Steppe buzzards take to the air from posts planted among the vines to encourage the local birdlife. In addition to the buzzards, Cape and spotted eagle-owls and barn owls are among the species that help keep vineyard pests at bay. By 2000, Gary and Kathy's son

JORDAN

Alexander had compiled a checklist of more than 100 bird species – and he's still counting. A copy of the list is available in the tasting room.

Further along the track you'll come to the vineyards that produce Jordan's great reds: Shiraz, Cabernet Sauvignon and Merlot. The best barrels of the last two are selected for Cobblers Hill, Jordan's flagship blend named in homage to Ted Jordan's previous life as the man behind a well-known South African footwear business.

Evidence of the Jordans' commitment to conserving fynbos is all around, and you may even see a rhebok, Cape grysbok or steenbok. The farm relies solely on water from two natural springs and its dams are rich in birdlife – the evocative call of the African fish eagle is often heard. Jordan's Chameleon range of easy-drinking wines is named after the rare Cape dwarf chameleon, which is now thriving on the farm after being protected by the family for years.

The cellar tour brings to light the equipment Gary and Kathy have designed to facilitate the gentle handling of grapes and wine. Here you can try Jordan's barrel-fermented whites (Sauvignon Blanc, Chenin Blanc and Chardonnay), which are something of a speciality, and a few of the reds too. In the hushed underground Chardonnay barrel room, try putting your ear to a bunghole and you'll hear the wine fermenting. Each barrel is rolled regularly during the *bâtonnage* process so that the Chardonnay is gently shaken (not stirred, as Gary quips) while on its lees.

Through plate-glass windows in the tasting room you can observe the workings of the cellar, or you may prefer to settle into a comfortable leather sofa to watch an audio-visual presentation of a year on the farm. Wooden tables and benches are laid out beneath plane trees and you're welcome to bring a picnic – but only until the Chameleon Restaurant and Deli opens its doors in spring 2009 to offer Mediterranean fare and farm-fresh produce.

Don't miss... a visit to the Thameside restaurant High Timber when you are next in London. Co-owned by the Jordans and South African restaurateur Neleen Strauss, it specialises in meat dishes accompanied by wines from its 40 000-bottle cellar – including Jordan, of course. You'll find it at 8 High Timber Street, London EC4V 3PA; *www.hightimber.com*; tel. (+44-20) 7248 1777.

PREVIOUS SPREAD A *soupçon* of chilled Jordan Sauvignon Blanc usually accompanies your early-morning view down the Stellenboschkloof.

THIS SPREAD Going the whole nine yards to ensure healthy grapes.

Chameleon Restaurant and Deli being built overlooking the dam.

Jordan is renowned for its meticulous vineyard management.

Gary Jordan monitors his barrel-fermented Chardonnay.

A percentage of proceeds from wine sales helps fund research on the Cape dwarf chameleon.

details

🍷 **Wine tasting/sales:** Mon-Sun 9:30 am-4.30 pm. Closed Easter Friday-Monday, 25 December and 1 January. Tasting cost: R15 (refunded on purchase).

🛢 **Cellar/vineyard tours:** by appointment only.

🍽 **Restaurant:** Chameleon Restaurant and Deli opening spring 2009.

👫 **Children:** lawns, birdwatching, chameleon spotting.

☎ **Tel:** (+27-21) 881 3441.

🖱 **Website:** *www.jordanwines.com*

MIDDELVLEI

Papegaaiberg

The Momberg family (and other animals) are a joy to
visit on this old Cape farm, renowned for its seminal reds.
Escape the madding crowd in this tranquil dell.

In 1919, when brothers Tinnie and Niels Momberg bought Middelvlei and pressed their first grapes for mainly fortified sweet dessert wines, the farm lay in the heart of rural Stellenbosch. Today it's the last bastion against suburban sprawl on the southern side of the Papegaaiberg.

Elegant white gateposts and a red brick road welcome you to what is still the home of the Momberg family, four generations and almost a century later. The farmstead, nestled in a dip and surrounded by pasture and 130 hectares of undulating vineyards, forms part of Devon Valley, whose south-, southeast- and southwest-facing slopes of clay-based decomposed granite soils are renowned for red wine.

The furrows that slow you down at regular intervals are placed, one suspects, not just to guide run-off water down the slope or protect children and the animals of a much-loved menagerie. They are a gentle reminder to stop and smell the roses – or marvel at the wonderfully gnarly stems of the decades-old Sauvignon Blanc vines on your right. Thought to be on their last legs, they have surprised with some excellent fruit after a stern 'farewell prune' by winemaker Tinnie, whose home overlooks this patch. Although more Sauvignon Blanc is being planted, the only white wine currently being bottled is a fresh unoaked Chardonnay. About 30 per cent of the farm's wine goes in bulk to the large producer/wholesaler, Distell.

Older brother Ben, a qualified viticulturist whose gregarious nature charms visitors and buyers alike, and Jeanneret, his equally vivacious wife, live in the Edwardian–Victorian main house. The *stoep* and rambling garden overlook the sprawling 1940s cellar and the cosy tasting room next to the farm dam. Jeanneret is the dynamo behind national sales and marketing, as well as a thriving export market.

You're likely to encounter at least one Momberg during your visit. Ben and Jeanneret (or her assistant Althea) will be in the tasting room. Tinnie prefers to remain in the vineyards or cellar, although he or his long-time assistant Thysie (who grew up on the farm) may take you round the cellar and allow you to taste some of the reds maturing in barrel.

The tasting room, a converted stable, is comfortable and casual, with polished wooden tables and *riempie* chairs. You can sit on the verandah in summer or in front of a roaring fire in winter – an ideal time to taste Middelvlei's reds. 'Stiljan' Momberg established the farm's reputation for Pinotage from the 1960s onwards and it is still the most planted variety now that sons Ben and Tinnie are in charge, with an exciting new fruit-driven Pinotage being made purely from free-run juice. The Shiraz and Cabernet Sauvignon plantings are turning out excellent wines too, as single-varietal bottlings or blended with Merlot and Pinotage. A juicy Pinotage–Merlot mix has proved particularly popular, giving rise to another easy-drinking red that combines Merlot and Shiraz and is called Red Falcon, after the bird on the family crest. For Tinnie, a long-held dream was realised in 2005, when vines gradually replanted over many years finally matured, enabling him to put together his ultimate flagship red blend. It's simply called Momberg.

The Mombergs are a tight-knit family and devoted to the farm and winemaking. Even affable 'Stiljan', although semi-retired, is still involved. Always ready with a joke or anecdote, he's the one behind the farm's quirky collection of animals, from dwarf Angora goats, wallabies, giant tortoises and pot-bellied pigs to donkeys, birds and dogs. Son Ben is similarly besotted, having nursed several litters of orphaned Cape fox pups discovered in neighbours' vineyards over the years. Pontac, the champagne-coloured *boerboel*, is likely to come and flop down at your feet, while Polla, the black pot-bellied pig, keeps everyone entertained by constantly escaping from his encampment to 'hunt for truffles' in a certain spot next to the tasting room.

PREVIOUS SPREAD Middelvlei vineyards cover the undulating hills on the southern side of the Papegaaiberg, with views of Stellenbosch and the Helderberg.

THIS SPREAD Gnarled old Sauvignon Blanc vines bounced back after a severe 'farewell' prune.

Three generations of Mombergs: patriarch 'Stiljan' Momberg with sons Tinnie and Ben and their children.

Jeanneret introduces young wine lovers to Middelvlei's famous reds.

Winemaker Tinnie siphons up some Cabernet to taste.

The 1940s cellar and tiny tasting room nestle in a dell.

Don't miss... a pre-booked Wednesday evening *snoek* braai with the family and other guests, or a summer sunset tractor-trailer trip, with a snack pack and bottle of wine, through the vineyards to a solitary stone pine with panoramic views.

The Mombergs are a tight-knit family and devoted to the farm and winemaking

details

🍷 **Wine tasting/sales:** Mon-Sat 10 am-4.30 pm. Tasting cost: R15.

🛢 **Cellar tour/barrel tasting:** by appointment.

🍽 **Functions:** small conferences in the loft above the tasting room (order homemade snacks in advance).

👫 **Children:** lawns, and pens and paddocks of farm and exotic animals.

ⓘ **In addition:** Wednesday evening *snoek* braais with the family (order in advance), sunset tractor-trailer rides through the vineyards in summer, with snack pack and wine, and WWF-SA vineyard walks (permits available from Sugarbird Manor, tel. (+27-21) 865 2313, or Stellenbosch Tourism Information Bureau, tel. (+27-21) 883 3584).

☎ **Tel:** (+27-21) 883 2565.

🖱 **Website:** *www.middelvlei.co.za*

KLEINE ZALZE
Stellenbosch

Scenic and immaculate, this farm offers
award-winning wine, acclaimed cuisine,
luxurious accommodation and a round
of golf on a professional course, all with
good old down-home hospitality.

Large chalkboard menus list dishes of the day, such as prawn risotto, slow-roasted pork belly and springbok loin in red wine sauce

Don't miss... taking your pre-dinner glass of wine down to the river at the bottom of the garden and watching the setting sun turn the mountains pink. You may hear the call of an African fish eagle or spot an eagle-owl in the oaks.

PREVIOUS SPREAD Terroir Restaurant's food is based on classical French cuisine, but leavened by Mediterranean, Eastern and traditional Cape influences with local fresh, seasonal produce.

Sunset tinges the farm's tranquil surrounds with pink.

THIS SPREAD Lush vineyards keep residential sprawl at bay.

The winery is linked to the tasting room and restaurant by manicured gardens.

Attentive service at the rim-flow pool overlooking the golf course.

Well-versed staff conduct formal tastings on request.

The Lodge offers scenic views of vines and fairways.

Kleine Zalze may be part of a whole winelands lifestyle package – residential estate, 18-hole golf course, four-star luxury lodge, winery and restaurant – but essentially it is all about enjoying fine wine and food.

In the late 1600s Kleine Zalze was part of one of several large freeholdings along the Blaauwklippen River that runs through the foothills of the Stellenbosch mountains. Although its neighbours had long histories as illustrious wine producers, the farm's own viticultural potential was only realised under the ownership of wine and spirit producer/wholesaler Gilbeys towards the end of the 20th century. Even so, when attorney Kobus Basson and his partners bought the farm and adjoining land in 1996, the Klein Zalze winery and vineyards were dilapidated and its wines were barely known.

Basson recalls that even as a student at Stellenbosch University he had an interest in wine and would take holiday jobs in local tasting rooms and hoard cases of wine under his bed. But, he says, it was ex-Springbok rugby hero and legendary vintner Jan 'Boland' Coetzee who inspired his love of wine as an integral part of enjoying fine food. And it was Coetzee who acted as consultant when Basson modernised the Kleine Zalze winery and earmarked 120 of the farm's 280 hectares as prime vineyard land. Some 80 hectares have been replanted to new clones of mainly classic reds such as Cabernet Sauvignon, Merlot and Shiraz, while Chenin Blanc from mature bush vines and Sauvignon Blanc from cool-climate Walker Bay and Darling vineyards also find their way into the cellar. Winemaker Johan Joubert makes three tiers of wines: the limited Family Reserve bottlings of exceptional wine in certain vintages only; the Vineyard Selection of premium wines fermented and matured in barrels; and the larger Cellar Selection range of easy-drinking, good-value wines.

Top South African chef Michael Broughton came on board in 2004, opening Terroir Restaurant next to the cellar and tasting room. Rated one of the country's finest dining establishments, it blends gourmet food with a relaxed, informal dining environment. Set on a long, wide terrace overlooking tree-shaded lawns running down to the river, it offers indoor and alfresco dining, with private balconies for intimate twosomes and patio tables under umbrellas. Large chalkboard menus list dishes of the day, such as prawn risotto, slow-roasted pork belly and springbok loin in red wine sauce.

Before ordering, wander across the patio to the tasting room to select a Kleine Zalze wine to enjoy with your meal. Broughton cooks with the wines in mind and both his staff and the tasting room assistants are on hand to advise. The winelist includes a small selection of other top South African wines and carefully chosen imports.

After a leisurely lunch, stroll down to the riverside to watch golfers teeing off on the second hole of the 18-hole golf course. Designed by American professional Peter Matkovitz, it is one of only three in the world set among vineyards with a working cellar. It hosted the World Amateur Championships in 2006.

The Lodge's suites are tiered against the vine-covered hillside overlooking the golf course and the Stellenbosch and Helderberg mountains. Resident chef Nic van Wyk moved over from Terroir to create breakfasts (served on a deck overlooking the river), light lunches and dinners in the Kleine Zalze Restaurant. Lodge guests are welcome to take walks in the vineyards or hire a mountain bike. By preserving some 30 hectares of natural vegetation, rehabilitating vineyards and using only non-agricultural land for development, Basson and his team have helped retain the original integrity of land increasingly under threat by suburban sprawl.

details

- **Wine tasting/sales:** Mon-Sat 9 am-6 pm; Sun 11 am-6 pm. Closed Easter Friday, 25 December and 1 January. Tasting cost: R15 for 5 wines, refunded on purchases over R250.
- **Restaurant:** Terroir, open Mon-Sun 12-2.30 pm and Mon-Sat 7-9 pm. Tel. (+27-21) 880 8167.
- **Functions:** weddings, seminars, conferences.
- **Accommodation:** ****Kleine Zalze Lodge with gym, sauna, swimming pool, preferential guest green fees, breakfasts, light lunches and dinners. Tel. (+27-21) 880 0740.
- **Children:** riverside lawns, gardens.
- **In addition:** De Zalze 18-hole golf course. Tel. (+27-21) 880 7300.
- **Tel:** (+27-21) 880 0717.
- **Website:** www.kleinezalze.co.za

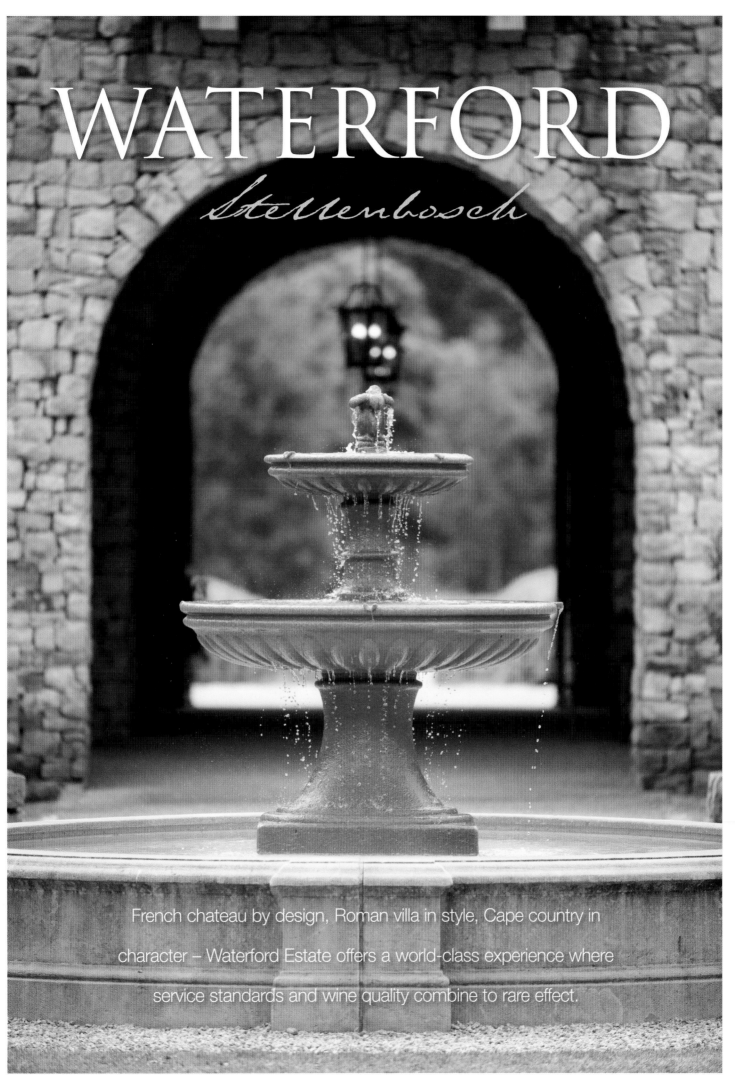

WATERFORD

Stellenbosch

French chateau by design, Roman villa in style, Cape country in character – Waterford Estate offers a world-class experience where service standards and wine quality combine to rare effect.

You finally come to two stone pillars topped by weathered urns and ahead is the winery, standing in a citrus orchard

Waterford is a gem. Tucked away in the narrow Blaauwklippen Valley where two mountain ranges meet, its beauty is a revelation. Driving along the wide avenue leading to the winery, you pass manicured lawns, natural lakes dotted with geese and cormorants, and a row of camphor trees along a ridge of boulders. You finally come to two stone pillars topped by weathered urns and ahead is the winery, standing in a citrus orchard. Designed by co-owner and vintner Kevin Arnold and architect Alex Walker, its biscuit-coloured walls, red roof, and terraces and archways of raw rock are complemented by doors, window frames and shutters in cool green. In late spring, the air is filled with the fragrance of citrus blossom and lavender.

For all its grandeur, Waterford is a home-grown family winery built on a budget. It was designed by co-owner and vintner Kevin Arnold himself, with interiors by wife Heather, with the aim of allowing visitors to share in the rarified world of winemaking. Essentially a steel structure with cladding, it is built around a courtyard shaded by plane trees, with Waterford's trademark fountain splashing in the centre. Tastings take place on the broad terrace surrounding the courtyard, where a young team of highly-trained assistants serve your wines from a menu. 'We discourage counter tasting,' says Arnold. 'We want you to sit down, relax and be spoilt.'

Each wing of the quad houses a section of the winery. Lounge on a sofa with your glass of wine and watch the harvest come into the fermentation cellar across the courtyard. Wander over to another wing to watch grapes being hand-sorted, peek into the dimly lit barrel room with its softly hissing humidifiers or witness the bottling and labelling process through large windows, shutters flung open. You may bump into Arnold, whose office also opens onto the verandah; you'll know he's around if you see two large Rhodesian ridgebacks lying on one of the kelims or at the open hearth in the tasting room. The Arnolds live next door and treat the winery as an extension of their home; Heather is constantly adding to the

eclectic collection of Cape country, French Provençal and Bali furnishings, spiced with the occasional ethnic African piece.

Asked by potential investor Gauteng-based IT entrepreneur Jeremy Ord to find a property suitable for wine-growing, Kevin and Heather came across Waterford in 1998. It was a sub-division, mostly under fruit trees, in a good viticultural area typified by deep clay soils. But its unusual position, encompassing two ridges of pure rock and pebble, promised something unique that appealed to Arnold. Having developed flagship red blends at Delheim and Rust-en-Vrede – and acquired a reputation as a top-class winemaker in doing so – he was aiming for a Cape 'Super Red' dictated by its provenance.

A decade later he felt he'd come close enough and in 2008 introduced The Jem. Named after co-owner Jeremy Ord, it's an unusual blend of eight varieties: Bordeaux classics Cabernet Sauvignon, Cabernet Franc, Malbec and Merlot, and 'Mediterranean' varieties Shiraz, Mourvèdre, Sangiovese and Barbera. You can taste it at a special Vintage Reserve Tasting, where you work through the evolution of this wine through six or more different vintages and varietal permutations, guided by Arnold or winemaker Francois Haasbroek. Besides being treated to 'library' wines (experimental bottlings that often earn selection for the prestigious annual Cape Winemakers Guild auction), you'll track the development of The Jem's vineyards, some 50 hectares that also include Petit Verdot, Grenache and Tempranillo.

Another extraordinary sensory experience is the Chocolate and Wine Tasting, the result of collaboration between Arnold and Cape chocolatier Richard von Geusau to match specific wines and chocolates. The results: Kevin Arnold Shiraz with marsala chai dark chocolate, Waterford Estate Cabernet Sauvignon with West Coast rock salt dark chocolate, and Heatherleigh Noble Late Harvest with rose geranium milk chocolate. A standard tasting of all the wines includes these three plus the Waterford Chardonnay and Sauvignon Blanc, as well as the Pecan Stream range of quaffers and a rosé.

PREVIOUS SPREAD Discover the synergy between tannins in the cocoa bean and red wine, as well as other fascinating flavour combinations, in the wine and chocolate tasting.

The Waterford wine symbol comes to life in the courtyard of this wonderfully interactive winery.

THIS SPREAD Raw rock pillars, an avenue of citrus trees and terraces of lavender prepare for a highly sensory experience.

Geese evoke images of the French countryside but there's no homemade *foie gras* as yet.

Co-owner and vintner Kevin Arnold.

The elegant barrel room, dimly lit by country-style chandeliers with grass shades.

The wine service is personal and impeccable.

Retreat to a courtyard seat beneath the plane trees where it's just you and your wine.

Don't miss... Arnold's one-off bottling of a Blanc de Blanc Cap Classique to celebrate Waterford's first decade.

details

🍷 **Wine tastings/sales:** Mon-Fri 9 am-5 pm; Sat 10 am-3 pm. Closed Easter Friday, 25 December and 1 January. Tasting costs: Standard tasting R30; Chocolate and Wine Tasting R50 (booking recommended); Vintage Reserve Tasting R100+ (booking required).

👪 **Children:** welcome, but no special provision made.

ⓘ **In addition:** guided vineyard excursions and tastings (to be announced).

☎ **Tel:** (+27-21) 880 0496.

🖱 **Website:** *www.waterfordestate.co.za*

VERGELEGEN

Helderberg

'I saw this estate with exceptional
pleasure since everything there
was laid out wonderfully finely,'
wrote Reverend François Valentijn
of Vergelegen in 1705. Follow in his
footsteps, as have Nelson Mandela,
Queen Elizabeth II and others…

'For 300 years only certain governors, slaves, priests, philanthropists, scoundrels, lovers, insolvents, peacemakers and murderers were able to take in the breathtaking views of Vergelegen… Now it's your turn.' These framed words remind CEO Don Tooth, long-time marketing executive Eddie Turner and cellarmaster André van Rensburg what their labours are all about. It is their task not only to realise Vergelegen's potential as one of the Cape's finest wine farms, but to place its rich cultural heritage firmly in the public domain. It takes a full day to absorb all Vergelegen has to offer, but it will be a day that you'll remember.

In 1700 the Cape's Dutch colonial governor Willem Adriaan van der Stel was granted the land on which Vergelegen, like Kubla Khan's 'stately pleasure-dome', was to be established. The grandeur of his undertaking – and the fact that public funding was used to finance it – were instrumental in the downfall of Van der Stel just six years later, even though the estate also functioned as an experimental farming, and viticultural, project. The farm's fortunes waxed and waned over the next three centuries under private ownership. When mining giant Anglo American bought it in 1987, it set out about resurrecting Van der Stel's original vision.

The 3000-hectare property is made up of forest, pasture, orchards, vineyards, gardens and natural vegetation in an amphi-theatre created by the dramatic Hottentots Holland and Helderberg mountain ranges. As you cross the Lourens River into the estate, you'll see the white cellar like a coronet on a distant vine-clad hill. A guided tour will take you through the vineyards to it.

A structural masterpiece, the winery is sunk into the hill and, to facilitate the gentle handling of grapes and wine through gravita-tional flow, it operates on four levels: grape intake on the top level, red wine fermenters on the second, stainless steel tanks on the third and the barrel maturation cellar deep underground. Its octagonal shape mirrors Van der Stel's plan for the walled gardens around the homestead below.

Only 170 hectares of the best viticultural land in this large land-scape have been earmarked for growing grapes: white varieties on the cool south-facing slopes, and red on the warmer west-facing aspects. The approach to selecting sites has been scientific from the start, and research into terroir is ongoing. The unequivocal aim is to produce benchmark Cape wines comparable with the French classics and modern New World powerhouses.

Some 40 hectares have recently been replanted in an effort to eradicate the ubiquitous leaf-roll virus: some 74 000 vines are regularly spot-checked and at the first sign of disease, the infected vine and its imme-diate neighbours are replaced. Not only has the re-infection rate slowed to a mere one vine in 4000, but the replanting allowed row directions to be changed so that wind effects and exposure to the sun on these high-lying slopes could be regulated.

A 10-year programme resulted in Vergelegen being nominated the first BWI (Biodiversity & Wine Initiative) Champion in sustainable, eco-friendly wine farming. You'll see evidence of alien vegetation being cleared on a large scale to allow the regrowth of natural mountain-side vegetation, and parts of Schaapenberg hill have been preserved to protect indigenous renosterveld. The small herd of bontebok beside the road heralds the re-introduction of larger fauna to join the small buck, caracal and other wildlife.

The tasting room, the gift shop and an interpretive centre with displays of Vergelegen's history and role in Cape winemaking are housed in three restored thatched stables around a courtyard. Taste your way through the outstanding three-tier portfolio of wines from all the noble varieties. The flagships are two red blends (Vergelegen Red and Vergelegen V) and a white blend (Vergelegen White) in classic Bordeaux style. The Reserve range carries mainly single-varietal wines as well as one-off blends, while the standard bottlings include the off-dry Vin de Florence white blend and the perennially popular Mill Race Red.

There is still more to the estate that Van der Stel envisioned in 1700. Much of it is given over to large trees and gardens: tea and scones are served on the terrace overlooking the octagonal Rose Garden; picnics can be enjoyed in the magical Camphor Forest; and the White Garden is the setting for the Lady Phillips Restaurant. In addition, a boardwalk leads through the fern thickets of the Wetland Garden to the Camellia Garden, a collection of more than 300 different species. And dominating all, on the lawn in front of the 18th-century Cape Dutch manor house, are five giant camphor trees that Van der Stel planted 300 years ago.

PREVIOUS SPREAD The 18th-century Cape Dutch homestead in its octagonal walled garden.

THIS SPREAD The 1816 winery converted into one-time owner Sir Lionel Phillips' library still houses his rare book collection.

Three of the octagonal cellar's four levels are sunk into a hilltop.

Pristine fynbos clads the slopes of the Hottentots Holland Mountains.

A 360° view from the submerged cellar rooftop.

A tranquil spot outside Sir Lionel's library.

Don't miss... the wing in the manor house devoted to photographs, maps and writings depicting the influences of the farm's five most significant owners: Van der Stel, the Theunissen family, Sir Lionel and Lady Florence Phillips, 'Punch' and Cynthia Barlow, and Anglo American. The assistants on duty can supply additional colourful anecdotes.

details

$ **Entrance fee:** R10.

🍷 **Wine tasting/sales:** 9.30 am-4.30 pm (sales until 5 pm) daily. Closed Easter Friday, 1 May and 25 December. Tasting cost: R30 for 6 wines.

🛢 **Cellar tours:** daily at 10.15 am, 11.30 am and 3 pm, or by appointment.

🏷 **Also for sale:** curios, jewellery, arts and crafts, books and clothing in the gift shop.

🍽 **Restaurants:** Rose Terrace, open daily November to April 10 am-4 pm. Camphor Forest Picnic, open daily November to April, pre-ordered baskets collected 12-1.30 pm. Lady Phillips Restaurant, open daily 10 am-4 pm; tel. (+27-21) 847 1346.

👫 **Children:** picnic includes children's menus, map and treasure hunt; lawns for playing and forests to explore.

ⓘ **In addition:** self-guided tour of the manor house. Gallery showing the estate's restoration and interpretive centre depicting its history. Sir Lionel Phillips' library. Garden and forest walks.

☎ **Tel:** (+27-21) 847 1334.

🖱 **Website:** *www.vergelegen.co.za*

THE LANZERAC HOTEL
Stellenbosch

A history of hospitality and an even longer tradition of winemaking have made the name 'Lanzerac' familiar to all those who appreciate the finer side of life. Wine has been made at Lanzerac since 1692, when Isaac Schrijver was granted the land in the fertile Jonkershoek Valley and promptly planted vines. The hotel, with the pretty Cape Dutch manor house at its hub, has been in existence for some 50 years, although welcoming guests to the estate became established practice long before that.

Thoroughly updated and with every modern convenience, The Lanzerac Hotel & Spa's 48 luxury en-suite bedrooms and suites – each with a private patio with views over vineyards to the majestic Helderberg – nevertheless retain an air of gracious elegance. Fine antique furniture complements the classic lines of Cape Dutch architecture, encouraging you to slip easily into a past era. How many hundreds before you have, after dining in one of the three dining areas, brought the evening to a perfect close with champagne, cognac, coffee and cigars in the elegant Craven Lounge?

The landscaped gardens, with their ancient oaks, invite relaxation, as do the three outdoor swimming pools and the spa. The picturesque town of Stellenbosch, with art galleries, museums and antique and craft shops, is just a few minutes away, while there are opportunities for golfing, hiking and mountain biking nearby. And, as you are in the heart of the Cape's winelands, there are many wineries to explore and wines to taste – beginning with Lanzerac's own.

details

How to get there
From Cape Town follow the N2 towards Somerset West, taking the exit to Stellenbosch/Baden Powell Drive. Continue to Stellenbosch on the R310 for about 17 km. At the T-junction after Vlottenburg Winery turn right, keeping the railway line on your left, continue past the station into Adam Tas Road. At the second traffic lights turn right into Merriman Road and continue through two more traffic lights to a roundabout. Take the second exit, then turn into the fourth road on the right. The first road on the left leads into Lanzerac Estate.

Who to contact
Tel. (+27-21) 887 1132, e-mail *info@lanzerac.co.za* or go to *www.lanzerac.co.za*

THE LANZERAC HOTEL (3)

MAJEKA HOUSE

Stellenbosch

The sleek, simple lines of the exterior of Majeka House give a clue to the classical elegance of this boutique hotel just five minutes from Stellenbosch. Within its white-painted walls, the restaurant is baroque-inspired and features a grand piano and an over-sized fireplace that dispels any hint of chill on a winter evening. The cuisine is understated and fresh, presenting a wide range of flavours. Changing daily and promising three different options at each stage, the three-course set menu is designed to appeal to the most discerning palate.

All the rooms – 15 in number, as well as a self-catering villa – are luxuriously furnished and equipped with every 21st-century convenience a guest may need, from wireless internet access to Lavazza coffee machines. Beyond their rooms, guests have more than enough to keep themselves entertained: perhaps a massage at the spa, followed by a relaxing spell in the Jacuzzi, a strenuous workout in the gym and a wind-down in the steam room or sauna; a swim in the pool indoors or outside, depending on inclination and weather; a browse through the library; or simply a pre-dinner drink at the bar.

A short distance away, Stellenbosch – the second oldest European settlement in South Africa – has much of historical interest to offer, as well as fine architecture, art galleries and museums, charming restaurants and coffee shops, and golf courses. Further afield, a scenic drive in any direction will lead to wineries that welcome visitors to sample their produce.

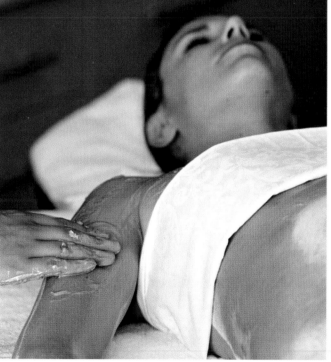

MAJEKA HOUSE (3)

details

How to get there
From Cape Town follow the N2 towards Somerset West and take the exit to Stellenbosch. Turn left onto the R44 and continue for 10-15 minutes until you see the Engen petrol station on the right and Stellenbosch golf course on the left. After the petrol station turn right into Paradyskloof Street and continue to a traffic circle, taking the first exit. Turn right into Houtkapper Street after a tree in the middle of Paradyskloof Street and continue to a stop street. Majeka House is on the right after the stop street.

Who to contact
Tel. (+27-21) 880 1549, e-mail *reservations@majekahouse.co.za* or go to *www.majekahouse.co.za*

CONTEMPORARY

Paarl

The Paarl winelands border Stellenbosch to the north and northeast, opening up into a broad valley with the granite outcrop of Paarl Mountain at its centre. Because the area is further inland from the coast, it is hotter and drier, with a Mediterannean feel, and it favours rich, spicy, fruit-driven reds reminiscent of the Rhône and south of France. But different soils and cool, high-lying slopes on the Paarl side of the Simonsberg also produce white wines of classic elegance. Although historically a winemaking area, the Paarl Valley has become home to a new breed of progressive vintners who are exploring new varieties and styles.

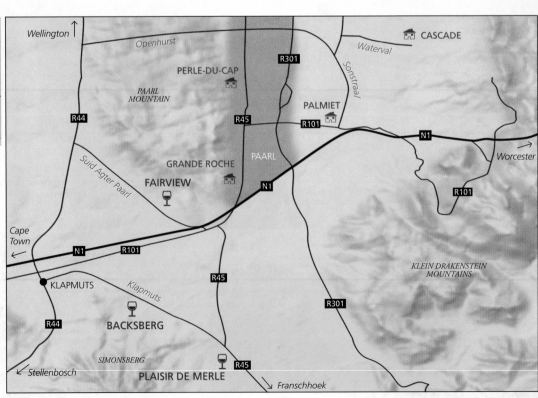

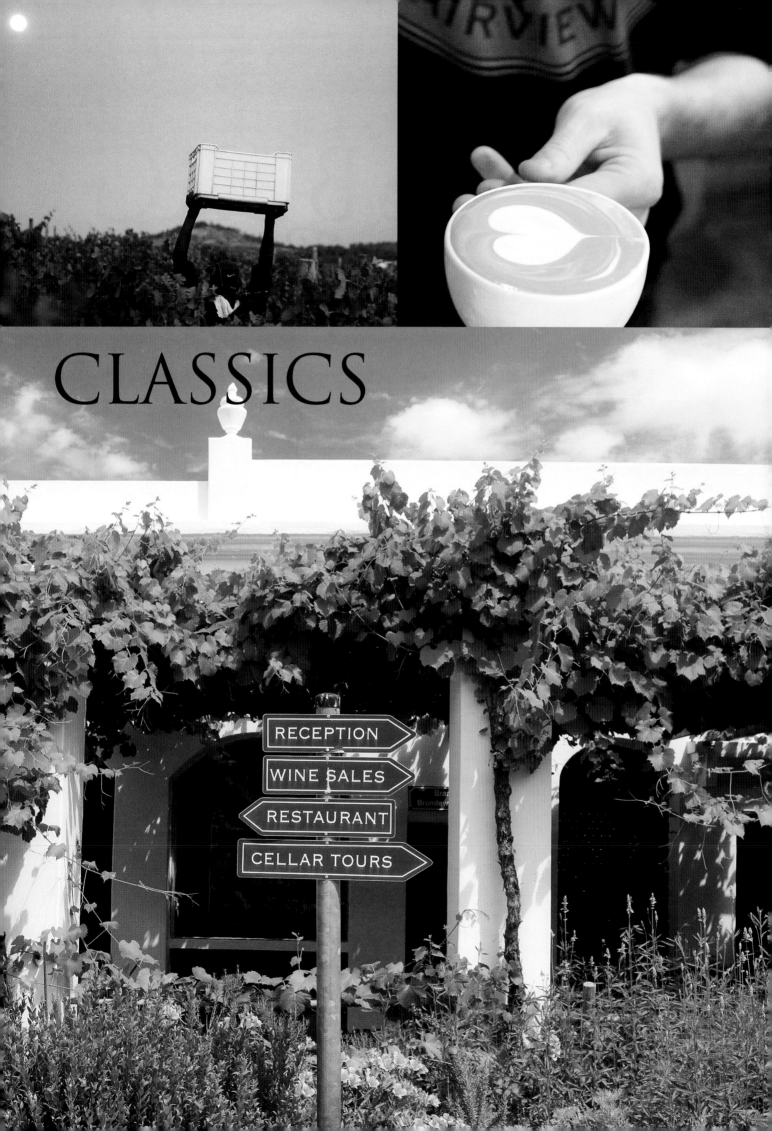

CLASSICS

RECEPTION →

← WINE SALES

← RESTAURANT

CELLAR TOURS →

BACKSBERG

Paarl

Groundbreaking eco-friendly practices underpin farming here on these Simonsberg slopes, a convivial place for families to share good food and wine in the great outdoors 365 days a year.

bushy-bearded son devoted himself to the vineyards. A pioneer in his own way, Michael started focusing on achieving the balance between soil, water, vine and berry that would produce quality wine; a new concept at the time, it is now a widely accepted practice.

Today, while the day-to-day winemaking is the province of Guillaume Nel, Michael still concentrates on the land and drives Backsberg's progressive environmental efforts. The farm is a BWI (Biodiversity & Wine Initiative) Champion, preserving 35 hectares of rare fynbos vegetation, and was the first South African wine cellar – and the third in the world – to gain carbon-neutral status.

The tasting room in the original winery, with its low wooden ceiling and wrought-iron hanging lamps, has the feel of a small-town general dealer's store. Cases of wine are stacked along one wall and individual bottles are displayed on hessian-covered wooden bins or nestled in wood shavings. Black-and-white photographs from the early 1900s show C.L. Back and friends, sleeves rolled up, pumping wine out of small concrete tanks. As you wander through, check the blackboards to see what's on offer: an older vintage perhaps, or a bottle of Pinneau (an unfermented wine fortified with the winery's own pot-still brandy). There is a range of Kosher wines as well, and South Africa's first Kosher sparkling wine is soon to be released. Through an archway you'll find antique winemaking equipment and a collection of awards and trophies from way back.

A long counter made of barrel staves is set up for tasting, or you can take a seat at a small table on the vine-covered patio. Starting at the top, the Babylons Toren range features Backsberg's exceptional bottlings from any particular vintage, be it a blend of reds, a Chardonnay or a rare single-varietal Viognier. The Black Label is reserved for vintage regulars that show exceptional quality, from the enduring Klein Babylonstoren classic Bordeaux-style blend and John Martin Reserve Sauvignon Blanc to the single-vineyard Pumphouse Shiraz and the 'Mediterannean' blends of unusual varieties, such as Elbar (red), Aldorina (white) or Bella Rosa (rosé). And then there is Backsberg's excellent regular range, comprising mostly well-priced, single-varietal wines.

Set in lush gardens, Backsberg Restaurant is a colourful haven where the house speciality, lamb on the spit, is a daily treat. A three-course luncheon is served under the trees on summer Sundays, while in winter the large interior is warmed by a log fire in the hearth.

When C.L. Back, a young Lithuanian immigrant, arrived in South Africa in the early 1900s, he started his new life as a dockyard-worker and delivery boy in Cape Town – and ended it as the owner of two flourishing wine farms. He bequeathed one to each of his two sons: Fairview to Cyril, and Backsberg, on the Paarl side of the Simonsberg, to Sydney.

At the time, the wine industry in South Africa was dominated by the cooperative system and corporate producer/wholesalers. Sydney Back was one of a handful of independent Cape vintners who turned privately owned wine farms into successful commercial enterprises, challenging industry conventions by establishing their own labels. Not only did they make and bottle their own wines, but they marketed them directly to the public, inviting visitors to taste and buy at the farm and sometimes even serving a humble cheese platter on the patio. Thus began wine tourism in the Cape.

This same brand of entrepreneurship has been passed down to Sydney's son, Michael, a trained winemaker and viticulturist who joined his father on the farm in 1976. While self-taught Sydney continued his pioneering work – planting Cabernet Sauvignon and Chardonnay, blending Chardonnay and Pinot Noir to make bottle-fermented sparkling wine, and distilling one of the Cape's first modern 'estate'-produced pot-still brandies – his reserved,

Don't miss... tasting the Sydney Back Five-year-old, Ten-year-old and Fifteen-year-old pot-still brandies. They're true to the Cognac style: Chenin Blanc double distilled in an imported Pruhlo copper pot-still and matured in French oak barrels. Have a nip after lunch at the restaurant (neat, or in a Sydney Back Brandy Coffee or a Backsberg Dom Pedro).

PREVIOUS SPREAD The Simonsberg slopes where vines are cultivated in tandem with conserving rare Swartland Alluvium indigenous vegetation.

THIS SPREAD The old vat cellar is perfect for private tastings.

The farm restaurant is casual and colourful.

Pre-dawn picking to ensure quality fruit means bundling up against the chill.

Wine shopping in the rustic tasting room.

The farm's extensive gardens are tended by a horticulturist.

details

- 🍷 **Wine tasting/sales:** Mon-Fri 8 am-5 pm; Sat 9.30 am-4.30 pm; Sun 10.30 am-4.30 pm. Open all year. Tasting cost: R15.
- 🏷 **Also for sale:** wine paraphernalia, fresh produce, bottled goods, clothing.
- 🍽 **Restaurant:** Backsberg Restaurant, open Mon-Sun for lunch; specialities are daily lamb on the spit (à la carte) and on Sundays a set three-course menu with spit braai and live music. Tel. (+27-21) 875 5952.
- 💐 **Functions:** weddings, conferences, seminars at Neville's Place @ Backsberg; lawn in private garden available for large groups. Tel. (+27-21) 875 5141.
- 👪 **Children:** children's menu, jungle gym, gardens.
- ℹ️ **In addition:** special annual events, including summer sunset music evenings under the oaks.
- ☎ **Tel:** (+27-21) 875 5141.
- 🖱 **Website:** www.backsberg.co.za

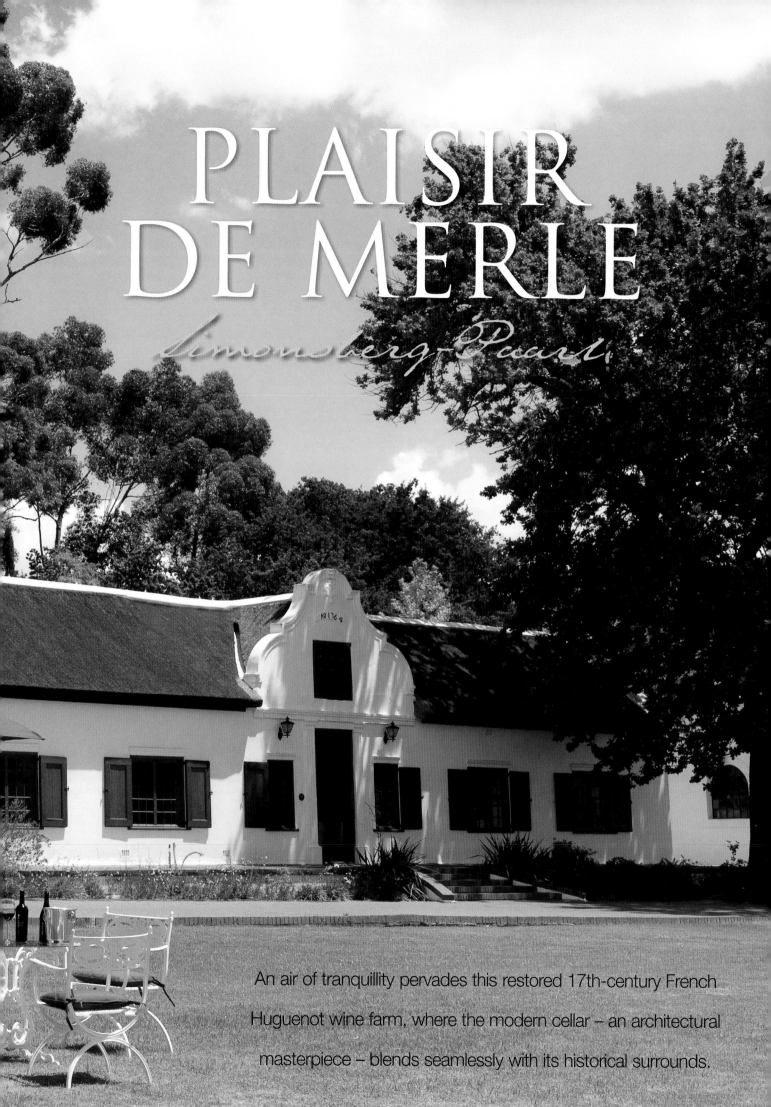

PLAISIR DE MERLE

Simonsberg-Paarl

An air of tranquillity pervades this restored 17th-century French

Huguenot wine farm, where the modern cellar – an architectural

masterpiece – blends seamlessly with its historical surrounds.

At nearly 1000 hectares, Plaisir de Merle is big – in fact, it's one of the largest single wine farms in the Cape winelands. It is also a winery of contrasts, where manicured vineyards that reach to the Simonsberg rub shoulders with tracts of unspoilt natural vegetation. In the same vein, although it is one of several showpiece historical wine estates owned by corporate wine and spirit giant Distell, it prides itself on its personal touch.

The guard at the entrance phones through your arrival, whether you've booked ahead or spontaneously decided to stop by. While driving past the lower-lying vineyards, look up ahead to the others that cling to the mountainside some 500 metres above sea level. As you park in the shade of oak trees, someone will be waving from the front *stoep* of the 1823 gabled barn. This is the tasting room, where furnishings are a stylish yet comfortable mix of Cape antiques, well-worn leather chairs and oriental carpets in warm autumn hues.

The wines are made from hand-picked grapes: Sauvignon Blanc and Chardonnay are followed by Cabernet Sauvignon, Merlot and Shiraz, and finally the Grand Plaisir red blend. If you're lucky, your hostess may allow you a taste of 'unlisted' wines, such as the recent single-vineyard Cabernet Franc made for the Swedish market. Exports account for at least 70 per cent of the Plaisir de Merle range and are vinified from a selected 80 hectares of the total 400 or so hectares under vines.

The style of wine is classic, and shows the French influence of both the farm's 17th-century beginnings and its modern redevelopment since the early 1990s. Vintner Paul Pontallier of Bordeaux First Growth Château Margaux – where Plaisir de Merle's long-serving winemaker Niel Bester gained experience – was influential in the early days of the revamp, which may explain the farm's enduringly low-key profile despite its wines' exceptional consistency of character and quality. Here, in vintage Bordeaux chateau style, it's more about the place than the people.

The original title deed to the property, dating to 1693, is framed on a wall of the tasting room and tells of the first ownership by French Huguenot Charles Marais, who hailed from the village of Le Plessis Marly (the origin of the farm's name). A 1710 sketch shows the scale of the homestead, the historical core of which you'll see on your way to the winery. You'll pass the gabled, thatch-roofed manor house, built in 1764, and next to it the long building that was once the shared living quarters of the farmer, his family and his livestock.

Built in 1993, the modern cellar is an architectural *tour de force* by Chris de Hart. Modern, hi-tech winemaking requirements fit seamlessly into the Cape Dutch farm environment, and at the same time the story of Plaisir de Merle is told in eye-catching design features. The building is set in a slope, its lower level below ground to minimise its impact on its neighbours: the 1831 gabled cellar on one flank and, on the other, the 1821 gabled *lynhuis*, or row of adjoining rooms, each with its own entrance. The new cellar is anchored by buttresses and surrounded by a sealed, stone-walled moat, and its domed roof is disguised by rounded mouldings with a gargoyle at each corner. A sculpted dove flies above each traditionally arched cellar window.

The main feature, though, is at the front, where a gently curving modern rendition of an early Cape gable sports a massive 'blazon' by sculptor Jan Corewijn. This magnificent frieze is a heraldic composition of symbols representing the history of Plaisir de Merle, its people and their family crests: a sailing ship, a lion, a horse, bunches of grapes, barrels and a crescent moon.

PREVIOUS SPREAD The 1764 Cape Dutch manor house.

THIS SPREAD A wide wooden skywalk traverses the elegant fermentation cellar and barrel room and leads out onto the original farm *werf*.

At home in the tasting room 'lounge'.

Gargoyle-like griffins spout roof run-off.

The sculpted frieze above the modern cellar door depicts centuries of ownership.

The stately manor house forms a backdrop to the vineyards.

Don't miss... walking around the moat to appreciate fully the new cellar's architectural beauty, and strolling across the vast lawn to the historical *lynhuis* to get a sense of the wide-open spaces that would have been familiar to the farm's early inhabitants.

PLAISIR DE MERLE

manicured vineyards that reach to the Simonsberg rub shoulders with tracts of unspoilt natural vegetation

PLAISIR DE MERLE

details

🍷 **Wine tastings/sales:** all year Mon-Fri 9 am-5 pm; Sat 10 am-4 pm (Nov-Mar), 10 am-2 pm (Apr-Oct). Closed Christian holidays. Tasting cost: R20, with tour R30 (refunded on purchase of a case of wine).

🛢 **Cellar tours:** by appointment.

🗨 **Functions:** small day conferences in tasting room.

👪 **Children:** moat, old mill house and large grounds to explore, but strict parental supervision required in winery.

☎ **Tel:** (+27-21) 874 1071.

🖱 **Website:** *www.plaisirdemerle.co.za*

FAIRVIEW

Paarl

Toast 'L'Chaim!' at this bustling Mediterranean-style winery, where the farm cheeses are almost as famous as the wines (and the goats are definitely as adventurous as the vintner).

1917

There is a distinctly Mediterranean feel to Fairview, evoked by its architecture, ambience and style of wine. And that is entirely fitting, for third-generation owner/ vintner Charles Back has been a pioneer in championing one of the Cape's strengths: its ability to produce richly fruited wines reminiscent of Italy, Spain and the south of France.

On a hot summer's day, there can be a wonderful air of somnolence about the place. Think Peter Mayle's evocative *A Year in Provence* or Chris Stewart's Spanish sojourn in *Driving over Lemons*. Set on a hillside dotted with gnarled olive trees, Fairview's winery looks across the undulating landscape between Paarl Mountain and the Simonsberg near Stellenbosch. From the oak-shaded car park, a cobbled pathway meanders across a lawn and leads up some steps into a sunny courtyard. Here you'll find the cavernous tasting room, its entrance shaded by a vine-trellised pergola.

Restless, searching, innovative, savvy, trend-setting: words used to describe Charles Back could also be applied to the award-winning and characterful wines that he and winemaker Anthony de Jager turn out at Fairview. Examine the displays in the tasting room that provide insight into the origins of some of the wines. Old photographs, snippets of information and samples of the different soil profiles – they all have a tale to tell. And, right up to date, recessed glass windows provide a view into the fermentation cellar with its shiny stainless steel tanks, revealing the business end of winemaking.

The Fairview label encompasses not only wines made from the farm's own vines, but also special bottlings from single vineyards and selected sites that Back has found elsewhere in the winelands. Each has a story: there is Jakkalsfontein Shiraz from nearby Perdeberg; The Beacon Shiraz from Koelenhof across the way;

Pegleg Carignan from some of the oldest vines of this uncommon variety in South Africa; Oom Pagel Sémillon, which contains fruit from Darling; and Caldera, a red blend from the Swartland. Back was so convinced of the Swartland's qualities as a wine-growing region that a decade ago he founded the Spice Route Winery near Malmesbury. It now produces internationally renowned blockbuster reds that can only be tasted at Fairview.

While exploring the tasting room, don't miss the display about the Agostinelli range of typically Italian varietal wines. It tells of Signor Michele Agostinelli, a trained agrarian who came to South Africa as an Italian prisoner of war and helped Back's father Cyril to establish a cheese-making enterprise in the 1980s, using the milk of Fairview's first small herd of goats. Today, Fairview is almost as famous for its cheeses as it is for its wines.

Although the herd, now numbering several hundred, is housed across the road from the winery, the traditional goat tower still stands in front of the tasting room. With its small family of Swiss Saanen goats, the tower has become a Cape winelands icon, not only appearing on the wine label as the Fairview trademark, but inspiring an anecdote about errant goats running rampage through the vineyards. This, in turn, inspired Back to form an entire wine company, which markets the highly rated Goats do Roam collection of wines. 'Herd' members include Bored Doe, Goat-Roti, Goat Door and even The Goatfather.

Fairview's emblematic goat appears in numerous guises around the farm and it's fun to see how many you can identify. A sharp eye may spot the goat's-horn embellishments on the iron balustrades of the steps that lead into the Beryl Back tasting room (named after Back's late mother). This hushed, medieval-like alcove – softened by thick drapes and the glow of chandeliers – can be reserved for a tutored tasting of Fairview's premium wines.

From the tasting room, stroll down the lavender-lined pathway to the former barrel maturation cellar – called The Goatshed, of course – for a convivial lunch. The fare is authentically Mediterranean and includes tasty bistro dishes, filled bagels and panini, platters of Fairview's cheeses and cured meats, and salads.

Don't miss... a visit to the cheese shop for farm cheeses, olives, olive oil and tapenades, and to The Goatshed deli for farm-baked breads and cured meats.

With its small family of Swiss Saanen goats, the tower has become a Cape winelands icon

PREVIOUS SPREAD A loaf of bread, a chunk of cheese, a glass of wine and thou: Fairview's gorgeous Goats do Roam reds are great with the farm's fresh Mediterranean fare.

Fairview's iconic goat tower with its family of Swiss Saanen goats in residence.

THIS SPREAD When the tasting room gets busy, retreat to the vine-trellised pergola or a shaded wall seat overlooking the tranquil pond.

Treat yourself to a tasting of Fairview's top echelon of wines in the secluded Beryl Back alcove.

Sunset bathes the winery and hillside vineyards in a soft light.

Feature plants include the indigenous strelitzia or 'crane flower'.

Aproned assistants man the counter in the softly lit tasting room.

details

🍷 **Wine tasting/sales:** Mon-Fri 8.30 am-5 pm; Sat 9 am-4 pm; Sun 9.30 am-4 pm. Closed Easter Friday, 25 December and 1 January. Tasting cost: tutored premium wine tasting – R60; wine and cheese tasting – R20; cheese tasting – R12.

🍽 **Restaurant:** The Goatshed, open daily 9 am-5 pm. Tel. (+27-21) 863 3609.

🏷 **Also for sale:** branded clothing in the tasting room; a range of award-winning farm cheeses, bottled olives, olive oils and preserves in the cheese shop; fresh breads, stone-milled flours, cured meat products, homemade chocolates and other speciality foods in The Goatshed deli.

👫 **Children:** welcome, but no special provision made.

☎ **Tel:** (+27-21) 863 2450.

🖱 **Website:** *www.fairview.co.za*

GRANDE ROCHE *Paarl*

Located in the historic town of Paarl and surrounded by vineyards, Grande Roche has many claims to fame, not least of which is a breathtaking panorama over the fertile Paarl Valley. Also renowned for its luxurious accommodation and award-winning cuisine, it has drawn accolades from many corners of the world.

At the heart of the hotel is the recently renovated Cape Dutch homestead of the original farm, which was granted to a certain Herman Bosman in 1717. This gracious building is now home to Bosman's Restaurant, where Frank Zlomke and his team of chefs provide a memorable fine dining experience. Nearby, Bistro Allegro offers more casual dining either in its modern, colourful interior or on the pool patio, while formal events, such as weddings or conferences, are also catered for.

Grande Roche makes an excellent base for exploring Paarl, one of the founding centres of the Cape's wine industry, situated in the heart of the Drakenstein Valley.

GRANDE ROCHE (4)

details

How to get there
From Cape Town follow the N1 north and take Exit 55 to Paarl. Turn left into Paarl Main Road (R45) and after 3 km turn left again (signposted Grande Roche) into Plantasie Street, which leads to the entrance of the hotel.

Who to contact
Tel. (+27-21) 863 5100, e-mail *reserve@granderoche.co.za* or go to *www.granderoche.com*

PALMIET
VALLEY ESTATE
Paarl

Situated in the heart of the Cape winelands, Palmiet Valley Estate makes a perfect base for exploring the vineyards and cellars of the Paarl Wine Region. A traditional Cape Dutch homestead forms the natural centre of this exclusive boutique hotel and, with a history dating back to 1692, it offers guests the charm and ambience of a bygone age. All the rooms and suites have been furnished with attention to detail, making careful use of valuable antiques to recreate the style of the 1800s.

When they're not sampling the local wines, guests will find much to do on the almost 40-hectare estate or in its vicinity. Some of the Cape's most beautiful golf courses are in the area and, closer to home, activities range from gentle walks to serious mountain climbs and from angling to hot-air ballooning and horse riding. On a hot summer's day, perhaps the best option is to cool off in the secluded pool or find a patch of shade under the trees. Weather permitting, breakfast, lunch and dinner are served under the canopy of the ancient oaks and jacarandas or on the terrace overlooking the aromatic herb garden.

Tucked away as it is in its magnificent mountain setting, Palmiet Valley may seem off the beaten track, yet it lies within easy reach of Cape Town and only 30 minutes from the international airport. With the best of all worlds, it is the perfect setting for a relaxed holiday.

details

How to get there
From Cape Town take the N1 towards Paarl and Worcester, leaving it at Exit 62A/Sonstraal Road. At the top of the exit ramp turn left, continue straight over two stop streets and then over a small white bridge. Palmiet Valley is on the left.

Who to contact
Tel. (+27-21) 862 7741, e-mail *info@palmiet.co.za* or go to *www.palmiet.co.za*

PALMIET VALLEY ESTATE (3)

CASCADE
COUNTRY MANOR
Paarl

Cascade Country Manor was at one time, early in the 20th century, the home of England's Duke of Bedford, and today it still has an air of grace and luxury. Built in the style of a Mediterranean villa, it lies, appropriately enough, on a 23-hectare estate of olive groves and vineyards. The fruit harvested from the decades-old olive trees is pressed into Cascade Manor's own olive oil, a unique blend produced mainly from Frontoio and Leccino olives. One of the highlights of a stay at the manor is a pre-dinner olive oil tasting, enjoyed with bread freshly baked in the wood-fired oven.

With only five double rooms, three suites and a family room to cater for, the owners of this family-run country guesthouse can assure guests of personal attention. The rooms are furnished in contemporary style, with an emphasis on comfort that generates a sense of wellbeing, and all are well appointed, with air conditioning and wireless internet among the amenities.

Olive and wine tasting are standard fare on the nearby estate, but guests may also go hiking or biking in the surrounding countryside, or try their hand at golfing or trout fishing. The Boschenmeer and Pearl Valley Golf Estates are nearby, and the Nederburg Wine Estate, for many years a mainstay of South Africa's wine industry, is worth visiting in Paarl. A little further away, the historical towns of Stellenbosch and Franschhoek, with their attractive architecture and intriguing shops and restaurants, make for a fascinating day trip.

details

How to get there
From Cape Town follow the N1 towards Paarl and Worcester, taking Exit 62A onto Sonstral Road and travelling 2.5 km before turning right onto Swawelstert Road. Continue for another 1.7 km and then turn right onto Waterval Road. Cascade Country Manor is 2.3 km further on.

Who to contact
Maika Goetze, tel. (+27-21) 868 0227, e-mail *welcome@cascademanor.co.za* or go to *www.cascademanor.co.za*

CASCADE COUNTRY MANOR (3)

PERLE-DU-CAP
Paarl

Paarl Mountain – so called because it seemed to early settlers that its granite rock glistened like a pearl after rain – forms a solid and peaceful backdrop to this luxury accommodation comprising five well-appointed suites. Each has a character of its own: Villiera pays homage to one of the leading wine estates in the region; Flamand has a touch of Victorian style; French pays nostalgic tribute to film stars of the past; Colonial remembers the grandeur of South Africa's Dutch and British past; and African has an earthy chic that is thoroughly modern. As hostess Kristien de Kinder admits, she has drawn inspiration for their décor from both her European heritage and a new esprit that she finds in southern Africa.

Surrounded by spectacular natural scenery and with views to the distant Hottentots Holland Mountains, Perle-du-Cap is above all a place to unwind and become rejuvenated. With both the swimming pool and the Jacuzzi fed by pure spring water direct from Paarl Mountain, there is an emphasis on the restorative power of nature. All you have to do is let it happen.

Situated as it is in the heart of South Africa's prime winegrowing region, Perle-du-Cap makes a perfect base from which to explore the country's top wine estates. In whichever direction you travel, you will find elegantly restored Cape Dutch manor houses surrounded by flourishing vines, welcoming cellars and tasting rooms, and hospitality second to none.

PERLE-DU-CAP (3)

details

How to get there
From Cape Town follow the N1 to Paarl, taking Exit 55 to Paarl Main Road. Once in Main Road, continue past the city hall and turn left into Mill Street. Turn left into the sixth street on the left – Carletta Street – and then turn first right into Tarryn Close. Perle-du-Cap Private Suite Estate is at the end of this road.

Who to contact
Tel. (+27-21) 872 0399, e-mail *info@perle-du-cap.com* or go to *www.perle-du-cap.com*

A CULTURE OF
Franschhoek

This mountain-ringed valley's celebrated French character comes from the Huguenots, refugee French Protestants who settled here during the 17th-century Cape Dutch colonial period, bringing a strong wine culture with them. Today it is a buzzy, sophisticated, multi-cultural hotspot for growing and making fine wine and food, with more eateries per square metre than anywhere else in the country. Its modern vintners, the Franschhoek Vignerons, are chasing wine quality by moving vines off the warm, sandy valley floor up onto the cooler slopes of the surrounding Groot and Klein Drakenstein mountains. And now, archaeological diggings have added a fascinating new dimension to the rich local history and culture.

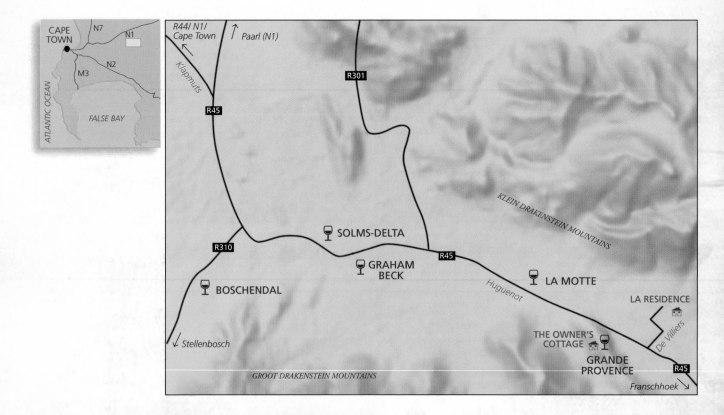

FOOD & WINE

BOSCHENDAL
Franschhoek

Exploring the rambling grounds of this grand old lady provides a rare glimpse of life on a 17th-century Cape Dutch wine farm. The pace is leisurely, whether you're sipping the latest vintage, taking tea, picnicking beneath the pines or dining under the stars.

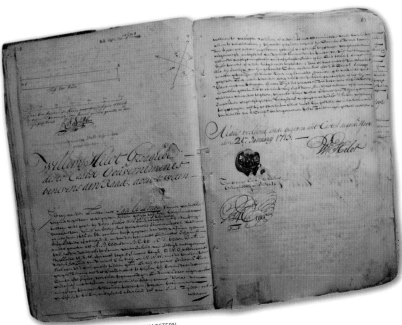

DAVID ROGERS/TITLE DEED COURTESY WESTERN
CAPE ARCHIVES AND RECORDS SERVICE

Don't miss... Boschendal's special occasions: Bastille Day in July; the November luncheon and sale of cuttings from the farm's famous old Cape roses; Valentine's Day sunset picnics; and midsummer formal dinners under the stars.

PREVIOUS SPREAD Boschendal's glorious king proteas.

The iconic Cape Dutch homestead dwarfed by the Groot Drakenstein peak.

THIS SPREAD French Huguenot Jean le Long was granted the farm in 1685, although he acquired legal title only in 1713 by deeds housed in the Cape Archives.

Flourishing pincushions celebrate dedicated conservation of the Cape Floral Kingdom.

The 1812 manor house with its decorative neoclassical gable.

Le Pique Nique's elegant picnic spot.

Winemakers monitor bottle development in the winery vinotèque.

Whether you come as a wine lover or a history buff, a visit to Boschendal is a pilgrimage of sorts. First granted to Frenchman Jean le Long in 1685, the farm was developed into a showpiece wine estate by French Huguenot Abraham de Villiers, whose family owned it until the late 1800s. Then, together with several neighbouring properties, it became part of the fruit-growing venture of politician and entrepreneur Cecil John Rhodes. When Rhodes Fruit Farms was taken over by mining monolith Anglo American in 1969 as part of its diversification into farming, Boschendal and adjoining La Rhone were restored as a single winemaking and historical entity. Today, Boschendal Wines belongs to wine and spirits company DGB (Pty) Ltd, while the vineyards, orchards and historical core of Boschendal are owned by a consortium of developers.

A good way to begin your visit is with a guided tour of the vineyards and cellar. From a viewing site far up the Simonsberg you can see the full extent of the property: all 2240 hectares of it, of which just 200 hectares of carefully selected high-lying sites are now devoted to vines. Fynbos is all around – Boschendal is a BWI (Biodiversity & Wine Initiative) member – and flowering stands of pincushions attract long-tailed Cape sugarbirds and brilliant green malachite sunbirds.

To wine lovers the winery is awe-inspiring. Part of Anglo American's 1997 multimillion upgrade, it includes a dedicated red wine production facility featuring a single, flexible ceiling block of concrete from which 42 stainless steel tanks are suspended. When full, they hold a mighty 880 000 litres of wine. Next door, in a cool, dimly lit hall, rest row upon row of French oak barrels: about 3500 in total. All in all, Boschendal turns out some 250 000 cases of wine a year.

Assisted by white and red wine specialists, cellarmaster J.C. Bekker produces an array of wines in different price and style ranges under the Pavillion, Boschendal and 1685 labels. The specialities, though, are Sauvignon Blanc and Shiraz, so make a point of tasting those. The Cecil John Reserve label is earmarked for particularly outstanding vintages of these two varieties, and although they're not available for tasting, ask in case there's a bottle open – or simply buy to take home.

Tastings are held in what is thought to be the oldest building on the property, a thick-walled, low-ceilinged barn dating from the 1700s. Or you can sit outside under the spreading canopy of a centuries-old oak and appreciate the wine, the beautifully restored La Rhone *werf* (farmstead) and views of the Simonsberg peeking out between the manor house and the early 19th-century cellar. A stroll through the nearby Exhibition Vineyard Block, where each of the classic wine varieties are nurtured, will give you a rare insight into the variations in berry, bunch and leaf size and shape. During harvest, freshly picked grapes are provided so that you can taste the differences between the varieties.

The Boschendal homestead is to the history buff what the winery is to the wine lover. The 1812 manor house, now a museum furnished with old Cape items reflecting Dutch, Flemish, French and English influences, lets you glimpse what life was like centuries ago. Take time out on a bench in the rose garden; peek into the fowl run, a cobble-stoned enclosure shaded by a magnificent mulberry tree; stroll up the oak-shaded formal walk; or admire the different styles of Cape Dutch and Flemish gables on the restored farm buildings dating back to 1802.

Today those buildings are home to Boschendal Restaurant, specialising in traditional Cape fare; Le Café, which serves cosy indoor or alfresco breakfasts and lunches; and a gift shop that stocks all Boschendal wines. And at tables set beneath a stand of magnificent stone pines you can enjoy Le Pique Nique – a basket of delicacies accompanied by chilled Boschendal wine.

details

- **Wine tasting/sales:** May-Oct 9 am-4.30 pm; Nov-April 10 am-6.30 pm. Closed Easter Friday, 1 May, 16 June and 25 December. Tasting cost: R15 per 5 wines; R6 per limited release wine (10% discount on purchase).
- **Cellar/vineyard tours:** Cellar tours at 10.30 am, 11.30 am and 3 pm, and vineyard tours at 10.30 am and 11.30 am, both by appointment.
- **Also for sale:** curios, jewellery, bottled produce; rose plant sale in November; sculptures at the open-air Shona Stone Gallery.
- **Restaurants:** Boschendal Restaurant, open daily 12.15 pm; tel. (+27-21) 870 4274. Le Pique-Nique, open daily mid-October to end April, 12.15-1.30 pm; tel. (+27-21) 870 4274. Le Café, open daily 10 am-5 pm; tel. (+27-21) 870 4282/3.
- **Children:** jungle gym at The Cellar Door, lawns.
- **In addition:** exhibition vineyard at The Cellar Door showing different wine grape varieties. Manor House Museum of early Cape furniture and artefacts, open daily 9.30 am-5 pm.
- **Tel:** (+27-21) 870 4200.
- **Website:** www.boschendalwines.com

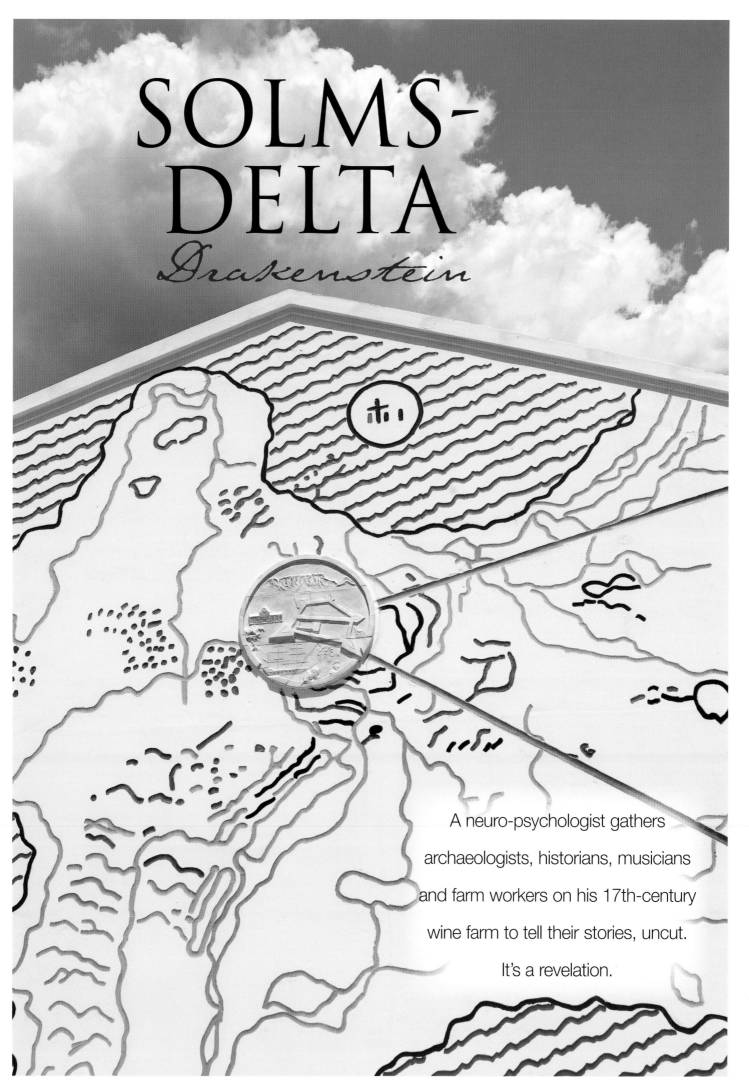

SOLMS-
DELTA
Drakenstein

A neuro-psychologist gathers
archaeologists, historians, musicians
and farm workers on his 17th-century
wine farm to tell their stories, uncut.
It's a revelation.

Next to the Dwars River at the heart of the Draken-stein Valley lies Solms-Delta farm, a remarkable place being developed by a remarkable man. Neuro-psychologist Mark Solms, from the South African branch of a German family with viticultural roots in Rheinhessen, has dedicated himself to telling the story of this particular wine farm and its people as a microcosm of life in the Cape winelands. And, quite by chance, this man's questing nature has led to the unearthing of rare finds that span millennia, resulting in the creation of a multi-cultural centre of community history in just five years.

The ongoing story is told at the Museum van de Caab, your first stop after driving down a dusty road among vineyards thriving in the ancient riverbed upon which the farm lies. Wine was last made here about a century ago and the museum is housed in a section of the 1740 cellar. Its earthen floor, walls of exposed river cobbles and red clay brick, and low wood-beamed ceiling are the backdrop to a fascinating depiction of the farm's history through meticulous pro-fessional research, artefacts and oral histories.

It started in the vineyards with the discovery of Late Stone Age artefacts as new vines were being planted. The stone tools, about 1200 in number, proved the presence of early mankind here, much as pottery shards provided evidence of subsequent settlement by

indigenous communities on the same site several thousands of years ago. The research grew to involve University of Cape Town archaeology teams and resident young historian Tracey Randle, who set up the excavation site of an early colonial abode between the tasting room and the 1831 gabled manor house, now home to the Solms family. Above all, the museum presents not only details of the farm's French Huguenot and Cape Dutch colonial owners, but a rare and complete record of its slaves, farm workers and other oppressed descendants of local indigenous communi-ties. The intertwining of all their lives is most tellingly revealed in proof that the property's second private owner, Christoffel Snijman, was the son of a slave woman.

When Solms came to the farm, it was the soil type and the hot, dry Mediterranean conditions that persuaded him and viticultur-ist Paul Wallace to focus on Rhône varieties (Shiraz, Mourvèdre, Grenache and Viognier), continue working with traditional Cape grapes (Chenin Blanc, Clairette Blanc, Sémillon, Pinotage, Muscat d'Alexandrie and Muscat de Frontignan) and vinify some unu-sual types (Primitivo, Tannat and Touriga). The first two groups contribute to the characterful, intensely flavoured wines under the Solms-Wijn de Caab and Solms-Hegewisch labels, while the Solms-Astor range comprises easy-drinking wines. In some cases, the ancient Roman and Greek method of pinching the bunch stem to concentrate berry flavour while retaining natural acidity, effectively producing desiccated grapes for vinification, has been revived to great acclaim.

Mark Solms' dedication to redressing historical inequalities and misconceptions and creating a new, integrated community with a shared past on Solms-Delta is evident wherever you go. The prop-erty comprises three separate wine farms: the home farm Delta, owned by Solms; neighbouring Lubeck, owned by British friends the Astor family; and Lekkerwijn, owned by the Wijn de Caab Trust with shareholding by the 200 people living and working here. The vineyards of all three are farmed and managed as a single unit by Nico Jansen, with experienced Cape vintner Hilko Hegewisch and cellar manager Fanie Karolus running the cellar.

History is everywhere at Solms-Delta, and even the Fyndraai Restaurant boasts an excavation site, eye-catchingly incorporated beneath the glass-panelled floor. The restaurant's main purpose, though, is to serve indigenous Cape foods, traditionally influenced by the sweet and spicy cuisine of the Dutch East Indies. You can enjoy the likes of *bobotie* (a curried meat dish), curried prawns, smoked *snoek* (fish) and *samoosas* indoors, outdoors beneath the trees, from a picnic basket in the riverside forest, or at a summer sunset concert overlooking the vineyards.

Don't miss... listening to *goema*, *vastrap* and *langarm* at the summer Saturday concerts featuring established and exciting new Cape jazz, gospel and folk musicians.

PREVIOUS SPREAD Fyndraai Restaurant, with its glass floor giving archaeological insights into expansions to the centuries-old cellar, celebrates local Cape cuisine.

Farm folk's perceptions of winelands history were recorded and depicted on a wall mural at the new cellar.

THIS SPREAD Riveting stories of farm life are told through displays and audio-visuals at the Museum van de Caab.

Mark Solms heads through the vineyards for his regular forest run.

Vertically trellised vines allow for the pinching of bunch stems to desiccate the grapes for greater fruit intensity.

The seriously styled dry Lekkerwijn Rosé in the Solms Wijn de Caab range.

A member of the Wijn de Caab Trust guides visitors through a tasting under a tree.

details

🍷 **Wine tasting/sales:** daily 9 am-5 pm. Closed 25 December and 1 January. Tasting cost: no charge.

🛢 **Tours:** wine and heritage guides on hand for cellar, vineyard and museum tours and forest walks.

🍽 **Restaurant:** Fyndraai Restaurant serves lunches, platters and picnic baskets.

👪 **Children:** museum, excavation sites, concerts; children's menu available.

ⓘ **In addition:** Museum van de Caab and archaeological sites. Summer Saturday Sunset Supper and concerts featuring local Cape jazz, gospel and folk music, 5-7.30 pm.

☎ **Tel:** (+27-21) 874 3937.

🖱 **Website:** *www.solms-delta.co.za*

GRAHAM BECK

Franschhoek

This is sophisticated wine farming, from scientific land cultivation to hi-tech cellar operations. But there's room for beauty too, as the farm's friendly folk share their appreciation of fine wine, modern art and cutting-edge architecture.

The Franschhoek cellar of Graham Beck Wines is probably one of the finest examples of contemporary aesthetics in the Cape winelands. To visit this winery is to explore wine as an art form – and to everyone here, that is precisely what wine is.

Owner Graham Beck first got involved in wine farming in the early 1980s when he built a cellar at Robertson in the Little Karoo (see page 140), and the Franschhoek property followed a decade later. Formerly part of historic Bellingham wine estate, it had been the birthplace of such famous 20th-century Cape wine styles as the Premier Grand Cru dry white blend and South Africa's first varietal Shiraz.

Beck's transformation included the replanting of some 70 hectares of primarily classic red varieties on the steep granite and sandstone slopes of Groot Drakenstein and a revamp of the existing cellar to specialise in white wines. It also involved the construction of a state-of-the-art red wine cellar. Built to handle increased tonnage from some 90 hectares on Beck's two Stellenbosch wine farms, the cellar broke new ground in aesthetic design. Johan Wessels, the architect of Beck's avant-garde Robertson winery, was briefed to combine the traditional with the modern. The result, with its sandblasted red-brick walls and multi-hued tiles, is reminiscent of Burgundy and Tuscany but brought right up to date with concrete trim, grey slate drywalls and expansive plate-glass windows. It is surrounded by rolling parkland dotted with massive abstract steel sculptures by Edoardo Villa.

The tasting room, guarded by a pair of Dylan Lewis bronze cheetahs and created by Cape Town interior designer John Zwiegelaar, is both sophisticated and convivial, like a chic nightclub. Recessed spot lighting plays on floor-to-ceiling varnished black and wine-red wood, gleaming granite floors and custommade bronze fittings, while jazz, swing or blues plays softly in the background. The difference lies in the tasting room's 'live entertainment': a hi-tech bottling line behind a plate-glass window – in a single hour you could witness some 3000 bottles being filled with wine.

Friendly tasting room attendants are on hand to take your order from the 'menu'. As an entrée try cellarmaster Pieter Ferreira's award-winning range of benchmark Cap Classiques (made at the Robertson cellar). Your main course could be a speciality of the Franschhoek winemaker Erika Obermeyer (whose acclaimed The Joshua 2006 won her the 2008 Woman Winemaker of the Year award) or a top-class red from any of the Graham Beck estates: the single-vineyard The Ridge Syrah; the Old Road Pinotage from 40-year-old bush vines; or the Coffeestone Cabernet from bush vines rooted in *koffieklip* (laterite) soils. And for dessert perhaps a Rhona Muscadel, named after Beck's wife, an art collector and keen gardener to whom the label pays homage with a line by Robert Frost: 'We love the things we love for what they are.'

There are several tasting options. The Classic, of five selected wines, is complimentary. A fee is charged for the Deluxe tasting of premium niche wines, but refunded upon a minimum purchase. For a slightly higher fee, a pre-booked Master Class features a definitive line-up of the top wines in tandem with complementary samples of fresh produce to illustrate the distinctive characteristics of each wine. The bite-sized morsels may include anything from local cheeses, *charcuterie* and chocolates to the area's own salmon trout.

Wines displayed from floor to ceiling are part of the tasting room décor. The back labels are refreshingly informative, so pick up bottles and read all about their contents. This is *prêt-a-porter* wine shopping in an *haute couture* setting, yet not too chic for bargain hunters. There's often a limited release or a discounted older vintage on special offer, or the Gamekeeper's Reserve Chenin Blanc and Cabernet Sauvignon, which are available only at the cellar.

PREVIOUS SPREAD The Groot Drakenstein foothills, where wine farming and trout breeding go hand in hand with restoration of the natural mountainside vegetation.

THIS SPREAD A pair of Dylan Lewis bronze cheetahs stand guard at the tasting room's Moroccan entrance door.

Cellarmaster Pieter Ferreira's 'office tower'.

Local artisans custom-designed furnishings in the tasting room overlooking the bottling line.

UK sculptor Stella Shawzin's marble figures recline among the plectranthus.

Old poplars shade the driveway.

Don't miss... taking time out to appreciate pieces from Graham and Rhona Beck's private art collection, such as the marble nudes among the plectranthus in a copse of stone pines, the intricately carved wooden Moroccan doors and Tamar Mason's beaded wall hanging representing Bushman rock art.

The tasting room ... is both sophisticated and convivial, like a chic nightclub

details

🍷 **Wine tasting/sales:** Mon-Fri 9 am-5 pm; Sat/Sun 10 am-4 pm. Closed Easter Friday, 25 December and 1 January. Tasting cost: Classic (5 wines) – free; Deluxe (5 premium wines) – R50 (refunded on purchases over R200); Master Class (pre-booked, with food; daily at 11 am) – R75.

ⓘ **In addition:** artworks and sculptures in tasting room and gardens.

☎ **Tel:** (+27-21) 874 1258.

🖱 **Website:** *www.grahambeckwines.co.za*

Although intensely private people, acclaimed South African mezzo-soprano Hanneli Rupert-Koegelenberg and husband Hein Koegelenberg cannot resist sharing their love of wine, music, art and flowers with visitors to their gracious 18th-century homestead.

As you approach the white gateposts of La Motte, slow down to take in the picture-perfect scene on the right: a tiny whitewashed cottage beneath a magnificent oak in a field of blue lavender. A date on a corner-post of the cottage suggests it was built in 1712. If an old powder-blue Volkswagen Beetle is standing there, Pietie le Roux is busy in the quaintest 'office' in the Cape.

Now entering his third decade as La Motte's viticulturist, Le Roux has gradually replanted what used to be a white-wine farm to mainly noble red varieties for La Motte's acclaimed Shiraz, Cabernet Sauvignon and Millennium blend. Now, on 20 hectares of marginal vineyard land, he's embarking on a relatively unknown venture in South Africa: the cultivation of lavender, thyme and indigenous rose pelargonium and *buchu* for essential oils that will be used in South Africa's fledgling perfume industry.

From the entrance, the drive leads past the farm's newer vineyards on the slopes of Klein Drakenstein and then past the historic core of the 18th-century Cape Dutch homestead. The white-washed, gabled and thatch-roofed manor house is but one of many historical features on the farm. Next door is the original cellar, dating to 1782, where the walls are lined with vats bearing the names of French Huguenot wine families who established viticulture in the Franschhoek Valley. Today the farm is run by Hanneli Rupert-Koegelenberg, one of South Africa's leading mezzo-sopranos, and her businessman husband, Hein Koegelenberg. Hanneli has added music to the mix, inviting leading South African and international classical musicians and singers to perform in evening concerts here throughout the year. At times she herself takes the stage. Pre-concert snacks and La Motte wines are served in the cellar or on the lawns adjoining the rose garden.

It's not only roses that bloom here. A collection of indigenous disas, members of the orchid family, flourishes in greenhouses under the care of La Motte's agriculturist Neels van der Linde. Hanneli bought the 30-year-old collection, the work of renowned South African horticulturist Professor Sid Cywes, to retain local ownership of this national floral treasure. Like her father, the late Dr Anton Rupert, she's an avid cultural and environmental conservationist. It was Rupert, an international businessman, who bought La Motte in 1970 to restore the architectural and viticultural integrity that French Huguenot Pierre Joubert had established on land first granted to a German settler in 1695.

Potted disas grace wooden counters and tables in the old cellar, which serves as a temporary tasting room. Besides winemaker Edmund Terblanche's elegant reds and an award-winning barrel-fermented Chardonnay, try the organically grown Sauvignon Blanc and the opulent Shiraz-Viognier under the Pierneef label. Grapes come from Nabot, a Rupert farm in the Walker Bay region that is dedicated to organic production methods and forms part of the Green Mountain Eco Route, a world-first biodiversity wine route in the Elgin area. La Motte is gradually introducing organic farming methods to its 75 hectares of home vineyards, too, which has helped to earn the farm championship status in the South African wine industry's BWI (Biodiversity & Wine Initiative). There are plans for a hiking trail through the mountain fynbos behind the farm.

The Pierneef label for small bottlings of exceptional wines originates from Hanneli's private collection of about 130 limited-print linocuts by early 20th-century South African artist Jacob Pierneef. Each vintage is marked by a different work. Previously exhibited in the formal tasting room in the cellar that has been undergoing extensive renovation, the collection will soon be housed in a dedicated gallery adjoining a planned restaurant between the old and new wineries.

Don't miss... a tour of the disa hothouses, which are a riot of colour during the flowering season, from October to February. Neels van der Linde is continuing the work of horticulturist Sid Cywes in breeding and cross-breeding this indigenous orchid from rare wild plants.

Potted disas grace wooden counters and tables in the old cellar, which serves as a temporary tasting room

PREVIOUS SPREAD La Motte's hillside vineyards and main cellar and tasting room complex, with the Franschhoek mountains behind.

THIS SPREAD Pietie le Roux's quaint 'office' in a field of lavender harvested for essential oils.

Look out for the National Monument plaque on La Motte's old buildings.

A National Monument, the water mill with its old millstones and miller's tools dating back to 1741, has been restored to full working order.

Winemaker Edmund Terblanche is delighted with recent cellar expansions.

The restored 1782 cellar hosts intimate tastings and classical music concerts.

Guests can enjoy food and wine pairings in the tasting room during season.

CHARLES RUSSELL/IPHOTOGRAPHIC

details

🍷 **Wine tasting/sales:** Mon-Fri 9 am-4.30 pm; Sat 10 am-3 pm. Closed Christian religious holidays. Tasting cost: R20 (refunded upon purchase of a case).

🏷 **Also for sale:** potted disas in the tasting room.

ⓘ **In addition:** monthly classical music concerts in the old cellar at 7 pm; tel. (+27-21) 876 4540 or (+27-21) 876 3119. Pre-booked disa hothouse tours; tel. (+27-21) 876 4540.

☎ **Tel:** (+27-21) 876 3119.

🖱 **Website:** *www.la-motte.com*

CHARLES RUSSELL/IPHOTOGRAPHIC

GRANDE PROVENCE

Franschhoek

Cape Dutch meets French Provençal and ethnic African in this

haven of fine wine, food and art. Three hundred-year-old Grande

Provence has been transformed into a chic winelands retreat.

Explore out back and you'll find a door leading into a tiny, secluded courtyard and an exclusive 'lifestyle' boutique

PREVIOUS SPREAD The Cape Dutch Jonkershuis forms part of a series of interleading spaces linking the tasting room, restaurant and art gallery with courtyards and gardens.

THIS SPREAD Grande Provence is the result of a re-unification after a 150-year division of two historic properties, once part of French Huguenot Pierre Joubert's original 1694 land grant.

The industrial-chic tasting room.

The magical result of recycled Angels Tears bottles.

The Gallery showcases the best in modern local art.

The minimalist garden provides exhibition space for contemporary bronzes.

GRANDE PROVENCE

Don't miss... the annual art exhibition 'Angels', which features works in all media on an angelic theme. Some of South Africa's finest established and emerging artists are represented, and often they have produced pieces especially for the event. It is usually held in December and January.

Dutchman **Alex van Heeren**, an international entrepreneur, fell in love with the 17th-century French Huguenot wine farm Grande Provence while sitting on the *stoep* sipping one of the cellar's award-winning wines. Grande Provence was added to The Huka Retreats portfolio (which also includes Dolphin Island in Fiji and Huka Lodge in New Zealand) and in 2004 Kiwi interior designer Virginia Fisher was commissioned to transform rambling old Cape buildings into a dynamic centre for lovers of wine, food and art.

Fisher began with the buildings' colour scheme: traditional Cape white-and-green became gun-metal grey with sparkling white trim and embellishments. The modern Tasting Room is all glass, aluminium and steel, with finishes in shades of silver, grey, charcoal and black, offset by white. The horseshoe-shaped, hammered-steel tasting counter is matched with 'barstools' made of steel posts and burnished tractor seats. Extra warmth comes from the well-used raised fireplace, not to mention tasting room attendants Ralton and Frances, locals who have been on the farm for years and will fill you in on its colourful past.

The compact, double-volume winery and 22-hectare vineyard are the domain of young, award-winning winemaker Jaco Marais, who produces a small, simple but showy range. The Grande Provence is the flagship wine, an uncommon blend of Merlot, Shiraz, Petit Verdot, Cabernet Franc and Cabernet Sauvignon. Its stablemates are modern expressions of classic varieties – Chenin Blanc, Sauvignon Blanc, Chardonnay, Cabernet Sauvignon and Shiraz – while the latest addition, a Brut Blanc de Blancs Cap Classique, is soon to be joined by a Muscat dessert wine.

Thus there will be a wine for each course on executive chef Jacques de Jager's menu at the highly rated The Restaurant. Situated just off The Tasting Room, this intimate, sophisticated venue is well suited to the contemporary international cuisine served in it. The Restaurant and The Tasting Room open out onto the Angels Tears Garden, a cobbled courtyard shaded by cream umbrellas and an ancient oak tree. Here, in summer, a marimba band contributes an African flavour to fine-weather dining.

Even in such sophisticated surroundings, well-behaved children are welcome to roam at will among the bronze sculptures in the Zen-like gardens and dabble in the fountain. Under parental supervision, they may even wander around The Gallery and, like the adults, cast an appreciative eye over the choice collection of contemporary artworks by some of South Africa's leading talents. Also opening out onto the garden, this gloriously bright and airy space is curated by Ilse Schermers Griesel for local and overseas art lovers and serious collectors.

Explore out back and you'll find a door leading into a tiny secluded courtyard (where more sculptures are displayed) and an exclusive 'lifestyle' boutique. Opened at the request of guests enamoured of the style of Grande Provence's interiors, it sells all kinds of gorgeous and unusual pieces representing that style, from teaspoons to tables. In the adjoining renovated Jonkershuis, Cape Dutch meets French Provençal in a delightfully eclectic set of rooms that can host wedding receptions, seminars and group gatherings.

Another of Grande Provence's tastefully renovated original Cape Dutch buildings has become The Owner's Cottage, named by *Harper's Bazaar* in January 2009 as one of the '10 Most Fabulous Villas in the World'. There are five luxurious bedrooms, an open-air elevated spa pool with vineyard views, and a conservatory for breakfasts and dinners (prepared on site by The Restaurant chef, who also provides alfresco meals in the pool-side loggia). And Sam, a charming young local lass, is in attendance should you by chance need anything more.

details

Wine tasting/sales: April-Oct 10 am-6 pm; Nov-Mar 10 am-8 pm. Tasting cost: R20 (refunded on purchase).

Cellar tours: Mon-Fri 11 am and 3 pm, or by appointment.

Also for sale: contemporary art at The Gallery; furnishings, crockery and jewellery in the 'lifestyle' boutique.

Restaurant: The Restaurant with its Angels Tears garden, open daily for lunch and dinner. Tel. (+27-21) 876 8600.

Functions: weddings, group celebrations, seminars and small conferences.

Accommodation: *****The Owner's Cottage, for exclusive use. Tel. (+27-21) 876 8600.

Children: garden with sculptures, children's menu prepared on request.

Tel: (+27-21) 876 8600.

Website: *www.grandeprovence.co.za*

THE OWNER'S COTTAGE

Franschhoek

DAVID ROGERS

Situated on the 300-year-old Grande Provence wine estate, The Owner's Cottage combines a sense of history with contemporary style. The boutique accommodation comprises four en-suite bedrooms and a luxury suite, a spacious lounge, a designer kitchen and a conservatory for dining. Step outside and you'll find a loggia in the well-manicured garden, a swimming pool and an elevated spa pool with a view across vineyards to spectacular mountains.

Tucked away in the Franschhoek Valley, Grande Provence was founded in 1694 by French Huguenot Pierre Joubert, who lost no time in planting vines. Today the farm's vineyards extend over 20 hectares of the valley floor, a gentle summer vista of green against the mountain backdrop.

With a wine farm literally on the doorstep, the first thing for guests at The Owner's Cottage to do is sample Grande Provence wines – created by winemaker Jaco Marais – and go on a winery tour. A visit to The Gallery and the Sculpture Garden, both of which showcase the work of established and emerging South African artists, could then be followed by a browse around The Shop, where selected items of small furniture and décor, health products and artworks are sold.

Since its major renovation and re-development four years ago, Grande Provence has been collecting an impressive list of awards, mainly in recognition of outstanding hospitality and service, but also for the cuisine of Executive Chef Jacques de Jager and his team at The Restaurant. Not to be outdone, The Owner's Cottage has been selected one of the '10 Most Fabulous Villas in the World' by *Harper's Bazaar* magazine.

details

How to get there
From Cape Town follow the N1 to Paarl, taking Exit 55 to Paarl Main Road/Franschhoek. Turn right and continue for 1.3 km before turning left onto the R45 to Franschhoek. After another 20 km you reach Franschhoek, and Grande Provence is the first wine estate on the right.

Who to contact
Tel. (+27-21) 876 8600, e-mail *ownerscottage@grandeprovence.co.za* or go to *www.grandeprovence.co.za*

THE OWNER'S COTTAGE (2)

LA RESIDENCE
Franschhoek

A secluded retreat with the stunning backdrop of the mountains surrounding the Franschhoek Valley, La Residence is situated on a 12-hectare working farm among vineyards, orchards and fragrant gardens. Space is the byword here: the balconies are generous and sunny, even the bathrooms are vast, and from every suite there are views of craggy mountains reaching to the broad, open sky.

All 11 suites are luxuriously furnished with fine antiques, Persian carpets and an eclectic mix of objets d'art, and some have additional – and unexpected – touches: in one, a marble four-poster platform bed that is heated in winter; another is decorated in Tibetan style, with Oriental antiques and hand-painted screens; and others come in the guise of French boudoirs. The chequered marble flooring and walk-in fireplaces in the dining hall and living room are reminiscent of a manor hall, as is the courtyard which, with seating for 120 people and an outlook to the mountains, makes a perfect venue for weddings. Rose-studded terraces and a gently playing fountain encourage guests to unwind outdoors on long summer evenings and to marvel at the beauty and tranquillity around them.

Days at La Residence can be pleasantly filled, with walks in the mountains or around the attractive nearby village of Franschhoek, trout fishing in the local rivers and wine tastings at the various wineries in the valley. Wine tours with a difference can be made on horseback or, more sedately, by horse-drawn carriage.

details

How to get there
From Cape Town follow the N1 towards Paarl, taking Exit 47 to Klapmuts and turning right onto the R44. Drive under the motorway and take the second left (R45) to Franschhoek, turning right at the T-junction. Approaching Franschhoek, pass Die Wynkelder and turn left into De Villiers Street. Turn first left into Dirkie Uys Street and at the end turn right into Elandskloof Private Road. La Residence entrance is about 400 m further on the right.

Who to contact
Tel. (+27-15) 793 0150, e-mail *info@royalmalewane.com* or go to *www.laresidence.co.za*

LA RESIDENCE (3)

HEAVEN ON EARTH

Overberg

Across the Hottentots Holland Mountain range over Sir Lowry's Pass lies a high, rocky plateau where timber plantations have long shared space with apple orchards. But its cool climate and mountainside soils have inspired vine cultivation in recent decades and Elgin has now also become synonymous with great wine. Cross the Houw Hoek Mountain into rolling wheat fields and sheep farms and head coastwards to Walker Bay, breeding ground of the southern right whale and abutting on the virgin wine territory of the Hemel-en-Aarde Valley with its ancient shale-derived soils. Overberg wine farmers' passion for wine is matched only by dedication to environmental conservation.

OAK VALLEY

Elgin

Friends of pioneering farmer Sir Antonie
Viljoen apparently 'severely rebuked him for
his incalculable folly' in buying this 'sourveld'.
But today's visitors salute his great-grandson
for unlocking its many riches.

'Aworthless bit of hungry sourveld in the unfashionable and despised Groenland' is how sceptical friends of Sir Antonie Viljoen described the nearly 1800 hectares he bought in 1898 near the Overberg town of Grabouw. How surprised they would be to see the flourishing orchards, lush grazing land, thriving oak forest and verdant vineyards on Oak Valley Estate today.

Sir Antonie was a local lad, schooled in Caledon, who went on to graduate as a medical doctor from the University of Edinburgh, Scotland, serve as a senator in the Cape Parliament and be knighted in 1916 for his peacemaking efforts in the aftermath of the South African War. But it is his farming legacy that lives on at Oak Valley, now owned by great-grandson Anthony Rawbone-Viljoen.

Sir Antonie's pioneering apple and pear orchards in 1900 were the foundation for Elgin's deciduous fruit export success today, and the 350 hectares of fruit trees are still the farm's mainstay. He also established its oak woodlands and, protected in perpetuity in his will, they now cover some 30 hectares. Although you'll drive through the woods on your way to the tasting room, they are also worth exploring on foot.

With 282 hectares of mountain fynbos under its protection, Oak Valley is a founder member of the local Groenlandberg Conservancy. It is also part of the Green Mountain Eco Route, a world first in biodiversity wine routes that promote an area's wines and its natural environment as a tourist attraction. Mountain bikers can obtain permission to tackle the challenging 23-kilometre fynbos route designed by winemaker (and avid MTB rider) Pieter Visser that has earned Oak Valley a two-night stopover spot on the Cape Epic mountain bike race.

Having established orchards and oak woods, Sir Antonie then planted substantial vineyards and built Elgin's first wine cellar in 1908. The vines soon made way for fruit, but were re-introduced on Oak Valley in the 1980s in a joint experiment with the viticultural research institute Nietvoorbij to test this cool-climate area's potential for premium wine production. The results were

Don't miss... BBC Channel Four's *The Devil's Whore*, a four-part period drama starring Kenneth Branagh and Emily Blunt. It was shot at Oak Valley, which, among its many other activities, has become a popular international filming location.

spectacular, winning acclaim for Hemel-en-Aarde's Bouchard Finlayson 'Oak Valley' wines. By 2003, with more than 30 hectares of carefully surveyed land planted to classics such as Sauvignon Blanc, Chardonnay, Pinot Noir and Merlot, Oak Valley was ready to launch its own label.

Sauvignon Blanc is a speciality, doing particularly well on the farm's cool south-facing slopes up to 500 metres above sea level, with Bokkeveld shale set on clay and weathered shale. The standard fruity Oak Valley and award-winning Mountain Reserve from high-lying vineyard blocks both show a minerality typical of this terroir. The 'Eskimo' variety Pinot Noir also thrives, and a new mountainside block of densely planted vines in true Burgundian tradition (10 000 vines per hectare instead of the usual 3000) should increase the quality of Oak Valley's sought-after Pinot. Vying for flagship status, however, are Oak Valley's two premium blends: a red (mostly Merlot with some Cabernet Sauvignon and Cabernet Franc) and a white (delicately wooded Sauvignon Blanc and Sémillon). Try any of these wines in the cosy tasting room located in a renovated farm building that forms part of this busy working farm's headquarters.

In addition to the Oak Valley fruit business and Oak Valley Wines, the farm has 16 hectares under cut-flower production, including five hectares in hi-tech climate-controlled Dutch greenhouses. Another 600 hectares is given over to pasture supporting a herd of about 400 Simmentaler breeding cows. Anthony Rawbone-Viljoen is currently busy with a new project to raise free-range acorn-fed pigs and an ultra-modern piggery has recently been commissioned for the purpose.

With 282 hectares of mountain fynbos under its protection, Oak Valley is a founder member of the local Groenlandberg Conservancy

PREVIOUS SPREAD Some 30 hectares of more than 4000 English oaks sadly cannot be used for wine barrels because quick growth in warmer climes results in overly porous wood.

Oak Valley's cool-climate vines lie high up on Groenlandberg.

THIS SPREAD Sauvignon Blanc and Pinot Noir thrive on cool, high-lying, south-facing slopes.

Bunching gerberas for market.

Anthony Rawbone-Viljoen and his winemaker Pieter Visser share a passion for wine farming in tandem with nature.

Some 282 hectares of conserved mountain fynbos allow indigenous plants like this restios to flourish.

Farm workers' children benefit from modern teaching facilities.

details

🍷 **Wine tasting/sales:** Mon-Fri 9 am-5 pm; Sat 10 am-2 pm or by appointment. Closed Easter Friday-Monday, 25/26 December and 1 January. Tasting cost: no charge.

🏷 **Also for sale:** pre-ordered hormone-free, pasture-reared beef by the half-carcass; other meat speciality products will also be available.

👫 **Children:** welcome, but no special provision made.

ⓘ **In addition:** walk through oak forest; three circular mountain bike trails, R30 per rider; no booking required.

☎ **Tel:** (+27-21) 859 4110.

🖱 **Website:** *www.oakvalley.co.za*

HAMILTON RUSSELL VINEYARDS
Hemel-en-Aarde Valley

Anthony Hamilton Russell's philosophy of 'expressing a sense of place' infuses everything he does here, including producing two iconic wines.

Wind your way up a farm road lined with cypresses and olive trees set among the vineyards

PREVIOUS SPREAD Beauty in both directions: the southern boundary of Hamilton Russell Vineyards atop the Raed-na-Gael mountain overlooking Walker Bay, and looking north over the Hemel-en-Aarde Valley from Braemar House's verandah.

THIS SPREAD The little cottage tasting room with the cellar behind.

Enjoying two iconic wines on the tasting room *stoep*.

The indigenous 'everlasting', whose papery flowers retain their colour long after picking.

A top Cape Pinot Noir matures in the underground barrel room.

Anthony Hamilton Russell and wife Olive, who's been researching recipes for a cookbook on using authentic local indigenous produce in classic dishes.

Don't miss... driving through fynbos along mountain-top Rotary Drive for breathtaking views of the Atlantic Ocean and southern right whales (some 150 in season) breaching in the bay.

Just over the mountain behind the town of Hermanus on Walker Bay – one of the world's top whale-viewing sites – you'll find the rugged Hemel-en-Aarde Valley. And tucked away in the valley lies the unassuming home of Hamilton Russell Vineyards' duo of iconic wines.

Wind your way up a farm road lined with cypresses and olive trees set among the vineyards. Beneath giant sugar gums stand two whitewashed, iron-roofed farm buildings. Next to them is a tiny thatched cottage overlooking a tranquil dam and a pine-covered hill. You'll be welcomed into the restored, hobbit-sized cottage with a glass of chilled Hamilton Russell Vineyards Chardonnay, its trademark elegance disguising a mouthful of fruitiness (with a hint of mineral), bracing acidity and toasted oak. No mere sip this, but a generous pour in big-bowled, designer stemware. Savour it on the *stoep* overlooking the dam (a good spot for birdwatching) or on a leather sofa in front of the hearth. Then try a glass of Hamilton Russell Vineyards Pinot Noir, famously endowed with fruit and tannin, and that distinctive minerality.

A wall-mounted map meticulously lays out the various vineyard blocks and an aerial photograph shows the farm in relation to the sea. Advertising executive Tim Hamilton Russell bought this undeveloped, 170-hectare piece of land in 1975, intent on finding the most southerly vineyard site in South Africa in order to produce the classic wines that only a cool climate can deliver.

When son Anthony took over in 1991, he started focusing on soil rather than climate, convinced that this was what set the farm and its wines apart. Extensive scientific soil mapping and separate vinification of grapes from different vineyard blocks eventually resulted in just 52 hectares of clay-rich, shale-derived soils being set aside. They alone would nourish the Chardonnay and Pinot Noir, Hamilton Russell Vineyards' two Burgundian classics, which were to be crafted by Hannes Storm, described as 'a perfectionist and a genius at the technicalities of winemaking'.

By your second glass, the unhurried air typical of Overberg farm life will have worked its magic. Come prepared: pre-order an Under the Willows picnic basket from neighbours Gillian and Peter, or buy provisions at the farm stall on the adjacent property, Southern Right. You can set out your lunch on the long wooden table under the trees by the dam.

Serious wine lovers are advised to pre-arrange their visit, preferably for when Anthony is taking a break from his international wine travels. You'll find yourself amid barrels of maturing wine in the cool, dim underground cellar, experiencing a vertical tasting of the three latest vintages of both Hamilton Russell Vineyards' wines. If you and your party give yourselves over to passionate discourse (and Anthony's not yearning for his cigar), he may uncork an older vintage, just to track the evolution of style or illustrate a subtle change in the oaking regime or a variation in vintages.

From there Anthony will escort you up the track to Braemar, his Georgian-styled hillside manor set in an olive grove. Lunch will be courtesy of his wife Olive, whose book of classic dishes that incorporate local produce includes *waterblommetjies* (Cape pondweed) in risotto and ravioli stuffed with freshly harvested *arikreukel* (periwinkles). She uses wild *suurvygies* (sour figs) in malva pudding (a traditional Cape dessert) and fragrant *kooigoed* (a medicinal renosterveld plant) in a mayonnaise for grilled line fish. Hamilton Russell's own fynbos honey appears in anything from sauces for crayfish to ice cream, while Olive's oil of choice is, naturally, the fruity estate-grown and unfiltered extra virgin olive oil.

An early supporter of the Biodiversity in Wine Initiative, Anthony has established a 38-hectare fynbos reserve on these mountains. It is home to several types of small buck, more than 120 bird species, bat-eared foxes and, recently, a shy Cape mountain leopard.

details

- **Wine tasting/sales:** Mon-Fri 9 am-5 pm; Sat 9 am-1 pm. Closed Easter Friday and Sunday, 25/26 December and 1 January. Tasting cost: no charge.
- **Cellar tours:** by appointment.
- **Picnics:** BYO or pre-order baskets from Under the Willows Mon-Fri 9 am-5 pm; tel (+27-72) 903 8998. Deli items available at Hemel en Aarde Valley Farm Stall on neighbouring Southern Right; also teas and light lunches.
- **Also for sale:** farm olive oil and fynbos honey in tasting room.
- (i) **In addition:** walks or mountain biking by special arrangement.
- ☎ **Tel:** (+27-28) 312 3595.
- **Website:** *www.hamiltonrussellvineyards.co.za*

THE MARINE *Hermanus*

With an outlook over Walker Bay and mountains all around, The Marine Hermanus lies right at the centre of one of the most beautiful landscapes in southern Africa. Yet Walker Bay's claim to fame is not the beauty of its setting, but the fact that it is where southern right whales come to mate and calve between July and December – and in doing so provide hotel guests with a rare opportunity to watch these fascinating marine mammals without leaving their luxury room.

In keeping with its coastal location, the hotel's aptly named restaurant, Seafood at the Marine, specialises in fish straight from Walker Bay. The open kitchen allows diners an insight into the constant activity behind the scenes while they themselves enjoy the far more laid-back setting of the dining area, where a wave-designed glass panel seems to float along one wall and subtle lighting, black and white photographs and glass sculptures keep the mood relaxed.

Seafood's more formal counterpart, Pavilion at the Marine, has recently been refurbished, with a new menu to match. Using seasonal ingredients to their full potential, the dishes reflect the wide range of local produce from sea and land, and are complemented by fine wines from the Bouchard Finlayson and Hamilton Russell wineries in the nearby Hemel-en-Aarde Valley.

Lighter refreshments – afternoon tea or evening cocktails – can be taken in the Sun Lounge and Bar, perhaps after a visit to the spa. In addition to other treatments, you can enjoy a body massage or exfoliating scrub next to the tidal pool, while listening to the soothing sea.

details

How to get there
From Cape Town take the N2 to Botrivier and turn onto the R43 to Hermanus. Continue along this road for 29 km, until it becomes the main street of the town. Follow it to the end, where traffic lights are situated on a sharp bend, and continue to the left. Turn right at the cross roads about 0.5 km further on; the hotel is on your left.

Who to contact
Tel. (+27-28) 313 1000, e-mail *reservations@collectionsmcgrath.com* or go to *www.marine-hermanus.co.za*

THE MARINE (3)

134

BIRKENHEAD HOUSE

Hermanus

Perched high on the cliffs of Hermanus and overlooking Walker Bay, Birkenhead House is a coastal retreat second to none, its beach-house atmosphere – with rare antiques, maps and art – complementing the beauty of its setting. From most of the 11 studio rooms guests can enjoy views of Walker Bay – and perhaps catch sight of one of the southern right whales that enter its sheltered waters every year to calve.

Two of Hermanus's best swimming beaches, lapped by the warm waters of the Indian Ocean, are on the doorstep, but Birkenhead House also has a split-level swimming pool and an infinity pool, as well as a gym and a treatment centre. Heading inland, mountain trails lead into the world-renowned Cape Floral Kingdom with its intriguing fynbos vegetation. Cliff-path walks are no less stunning, and a leisurely 40-minute coastal stroll will take you right into the town.

With appetites sharpened by the fresh sea air, emphasis is placed on the quality of the cuisine, and lavish meals and seafood delicacies are part of the daily menu. Breakfasts are substantial, and can be served in your room or on the patio overlooking the bay.

Space, light and water flow together in harmony at Birkenhead House, making it a casual and yet luxurious place to stay. And whether you enjoy being pampered or sipping a cocktail after an evening swim, you'll find that the fresh air, good food and endless ocean views have a definite rejuvenating effect.

details

How to get there
From Cape Town take the N2 eastwards and drive about 100 km to Botrivier. Follow the R43 signposted to Hermanus and continue another 38 km to the town. Drive through the centre to a traffic circle (about 6 km) and take the second exit, continuing along Main Road. After about 1 km turn right into 7th Avenue; Birkenhead House is 200 m further, at the corner of 7th Avenue and 11th Street.

Who to contact
Tel. (+27-15) 793 0150, e-mail *info@royalmalewane.com* or go to *www.birkenheadhouse.com*

BIRKENHEAD HOUSE (4)

GROOTBOS
PRIVATE NATURE RESERVE
Gansbaai

Luxury in harmony with nature is an ideal easier to talk about than to achieve – but at Grootbos it is a reality. Overlooking Walker Bay, this private nature reserve combines the comforts of five-star accommodation with an environment of conservation and human development. Central to the reserve is its 1768-hectare share of the much larger Cape Floral Kingdom – a share in which more than 745 species of indigenous flowering plants are protected.

Well-known British conservationist David Bellamy has described Grootbos as 'the best example of the conservation of biodiversity I have ever seen', and the Eden Project in Cornwall has adopted it as a major partner in its quest to develop its South African display and promote the link between people and plants. Guests at Grootbos are encouraged to explore the reserve on foot or horseback, or in a 4x4, and discover some of nature's more subtle nuances. Birdwatchers, gardeners, wildflower enthusiasts, whale watchers – they will all find something of interest.

But that is only half the story: guests will also appreciate the spacious suites with views of the dunes and ocean, private wooden decks and separate living rooms with cosy fireplaces. The gourmet cuisine is crafted from fresh local ingredients, including just-caught seafood specialities, and is complemented by excellent local wines. Enjoying a fine dinner while watching one of the most beautiful sunsets in Africa just goes to show that conservation, luxury and relaxation really can be brought together in perfect balance.

details

How to get there
From Cape Town follow the N2 to Somerset West and either continue over Sir Lowry's and Houw Hoek passes, turning onto the R43 to Hermanus, or take the R44 along the coast before joining the R43 to Hermanus. Drive through Hermanus and continue on the R43. Grootbos is 13 km past Stanford.

Who to contact
Tel. (+27-28) 384 8000, e-mail *reservations@grootbos.co.za* or go to *www.grootbos.com*

GROOTBOS PRIVATE NATURE RESERVE (4)

SCHULPHOEK
SEAFRONT GUESTHOUSE
Hermanus

Southern right whales are special at Schulphoek – you can either arrange to go looking for them from a boat or light aircraft, or simply relax in the guest lounge and wait for them to come into the protected bay while you're enjoying the sea view. And there is much more wildlife watching on offer nearby, from great white sharks to African penguins. A stroll through one of the two nature reserves or along a cliff path can be rewarding, while the markets, art galleries and antique shops of Hermanus are worth exploring.

The guesthouse comprises six generously appointed garden suites and a first-floor suite with spectacular views. Dinner is served at a social table in the seafront dining room, with menus changed daily to make use of the freshest local produce available – even from Schulphoek's own organic garden. A 12 000-bottle cellar supplies complementary wines.

And if you tire of watching whales, you can always unwind with body therapy or a dip in the salt-water pool.

details

How to get there
From Cape Town take the N2 past Somerset West and over Sir Lowry's Pass. After Houw Hoek, turn onto the R43 to Botrivier and Hermanus, and continue past Onrus. At Sandbaai, turn right into Main Road and left into Third Avenue, continuing to Piet Retief Crescent where you will see the entrance to Schulphoek.

Who to contact
Tel. (+27-28) 316 2626, e-mail *schulphoek@hermanus.co.za* or go to *www.schulphoek.co.za*

SCHULPHOEK SEAFRONT GUESTHOUSE (3)

FINE WINES FROM
Further Afield

Head across the magnificent Du Toitskloof Mountains and the vine-clad expanse of the Breede River Valley onto Route 62 for an entirely different winelands experience. This is rugged, semi-arid land with stony, shale soils (though it surprises in spring with the fragrance and colour of its avidly conserved tracts of fynbos). Here, as in the even warmer, similarly rocky, mountain-ringed Tulbagh Valley to the northwest, informed modern viticulture and progressive vintners have turned marginal white-wine territory into a source of great reds and classic sparkling wines. Although the wines are now as sophisticated as the welcome, visitors will enjoy the feeling of getting off the beaten track.

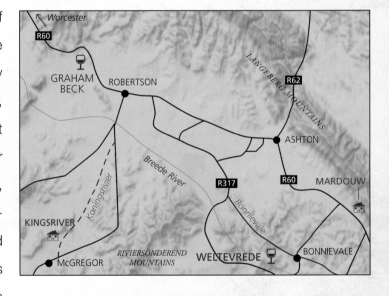

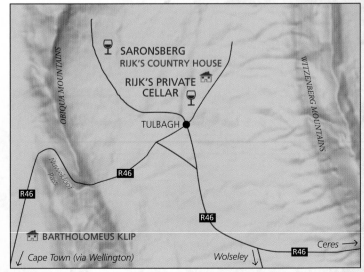

ANCIENT SOILS

GRAHAM BECK

Robertson

The home of world-renowned Cap Classiques and other acclaimed wines, this colourful avant-garde cellar offers a stylish respite on a trip into the Cape winelands' semi-arid hinterland.

When **Graham Beck** bought this Robertson winery some 25 years ago, his intention was that it would produce his flagship wine: a premium sparkling wine *à la Champagne*. At the time, both Cap Classique and Robertson's reputation as a fine wine area were in their infancy, but Beck, with the assistance of long-time cellarmaster Pieter Ferreira, successfully shook things up.

Having purchased the derelict farm Madeba in the semi-arid Little Karoo scrubland and then called in a fleet of earth-moving equipment to redistribute vast amounts of fertile topsoil swept away by the 1981 Laingsburg floods, Beck planted a range of classic wine grape varieties. Ongoing research and careful monitoring of the vineyards led to today's focus on Chardonnay, Shiraz, Pinot Noir and Cabernet Sauvignon, and limestone-rich soils produce grapes with the high natural acidity required for the base wines that go into quality sparkling wine.

The wines themselves are made in the avant-garde cellar that has been described by its designer, Johan Wessels, as a 'hi-tech alien egg [that] hatched in the fynbos on the hillside' – and its sloping green roof, burnt-orange walls and purple-pink steelwork really do echo the colours of the surrounding veld. The tasting room is modern and minimalist, combining polished steel, granite and glass. Its elevated deck overlooks the still waters of a koi pond and an oasis of lawns, vines and indigenous acacia trees, and at one end stands an

limestone-rich soils produce grapes with the high natural acidity required for the base wines that go into quality sparkling wine

Don't miss... an unofficial guided walk with Mossie through the Graham Beck private nature reserve. Phone ahead or plan around the Robertson Wine Valley's annual Wacky Wine Weekend (June) or Slow Festival (August).

PREVIOUS SPREAD One of the Cape's consistently high-quality bubblies stacked in a pupitre.

The avant-garde cellar in the rich colours of the surrounding soils, scrub and wild flowers.

THIS SPREAD An oasis of tranquil waters, lush gardens and twinkling lights.

Ebullient in-house nature conservator Mossie Basson, a man on a mission.

An Edoardo Villa steel sculpture.

Hi-tech winemaking in temperature-controlled stainless steel tanks.

A generous pour for a bubbly tasting.

imposing angular black steel sculpture by Edoardo Villa. There is no better place to sample some of the Cape's finest Cap Classiques.

Although the Brut NV is an excellent everyday drinking wine, it has greater claims to fame. In 1994 it was the sparkling wine of choice to celebrate Nelson Mandela's election as president of newly democratic South Africa, and it was drunk when Barack Obama announced his candidacy for president of the United States and when he won the election in 2008. It has also been awarded the WINE magazine Amorim Cork Cap Classique Challenge. But the flagship sparkling wine that Beck had originally envisaged proved to be the Blanc de Blancs, made from pure Chardonnay. Affirmation came when the 1999 vintage earned Ferreira the Diners Club Winemaker of the Year Award in 2004, essentially marking the wine as South Africa's best Cap Classique.

Other notable sparkling wines produced on the farm are Brut Rosé, made predominantly with Pinot Noir (which accounts for the trademark hint of a blush); and Bliss Demi Sec, a rare semi-sweet version made as a quality bottle-fermented Cap Classique that has a freshness and character seldom found in this style of bubbly. The most recent addition is Cuvée Clive, a limited bottling of a 2003 cuvée disgorged after five years on the lees, resulting in exceptional character and richness. Named in memory of a Beck son who died in an accident, it is only available from the cellar door at both Robertson and Franschhoek.

Although Ferreira says he's 'still in search of the perfect bubble', there is more to this Robertson farm than sparkling wines. The Ridge Syrah, from a single local vineyard on rich, red soils, is resident wine-maker Irene Waller's favourite variety, while the Lonehill Chardonnay is another local heavyweight. As is the case at the Franschhoek tasting room, the entire range of Graham Beck wines is available here.

While tasting, you may be lucky enough to meet Mossie Basson, Graham Beck Wines' full-time estate and conservation manager. Quaffing a glass of the new Rosé (an unusual blend of Malbec and Sangiovese), he'll tell you about the farm's 1800-hectare nature reserve. It's the hub of the Rooiberg–Breederivier Conservancy, which encompasses more than 13 000 hectares of natural vegetation and is home to the endangered riverine rabbit. And he'll explain that the entire wine growing, production and sales operation hinges on a five-point management programme that places environmental considerations first.

details

🍷 **Wine tasting/sales:** Mon-Fri 9 am-5 pm; Sat and Sun (Sun, Oct – Apr) 10 am-3 pm. Closed Easter Friday, 25 December and 1 January. Tasting cost: Classic (5 wines) – free; Deluxe Tasting (5 premium wines) – R50 (refunded on purchases over R200).

🛢 **Cellar tours:** by appointment.

☎ **Tel:** (+27-23) 626 1214.

🖱 **Website:** *www.grahambeckwines.co.za*

WELTEVREDE
Bonnievale

The Jonker family has farmed this stretch of the Breede River for generations and now focuses on distinctive wines born of what young winemaker Philip Jonker calls 'the Creator's off-cuts'.

Breakfasts, teas and light lunches are served outside on a patio beneath a trellised vine at tables decked in cheery red tablecloths

WELTEVREDE
Place of Rocks Chardonnay

Don't miss... a pre-booked guided walk with Philip Jonker into the Weltevrede Conservancy to see indigenous plants with such marvellously descriptive vernacular names as *voëltjie-kan-nie-sit-nie* (little bird can't sit), *bobbejaantone* (baboon's toes) and *skilpadskos* (tortoise food). Pack a chilled bottle of Weltevrede's vintage-fresh grape juice or, on a winter's day, Oupa se Wyn, a fortified sweet dessert wine.

PREVIOUS SPREAD The Breede River, bringer of life: Weltevrede is part of a privately owned shared canal system that allows farms to open sluice gates at allocated times to water their land.

THIS SPREAD 'Weltevrede, with its variety of different soil types, is made up of the Creator's off-cuts,' says Philip Jonker.

A pocket of shale produces Place of Rocks Chardonnay's distinctive fresh, lemony character.

Bottle-maturing Cap Classique stored in excavated underground old fementation tanks.

The farm's two guest cottages are set among the vines.

Philip and daughter Marianna, the fifth-generation Jonker on the farm.

The Jonker family is the heart and soul of the far corner of the Cape winelands that lies between the lush Breede River Valley and the rocky scrubland of the Little Karoo. In 1912 Klaas Jonker bought a few hundred hectares on the banks of the Breede near the settlement of Bonnievale, named it Weltevrede ('well satisfied') and in due course bequeathed a farm in the valley to each of his four sons and four daughters.

Young fourth-generation winemaker Philip Jonker feels keenly the farm's sense of place and his family's roots in this rugged landscape. He seeks to make wines that, he says, 'are a sincere attempt at expressing their origin in these specific soils'. Weltevrede is marked by a quirky geological profile that shows extreme variations in soil type, even from one row of vines to another. Samples of the distinctive soil types are displayed in the tasting room, alongside the wines they produce. Bedrock Black Syrah comes from vines whose roots push down to hard grey bedrock. Rusted Soil Chardonnay and Place of Rocks Chardonnay, although identically vinified, show remarkable differences in style and flavour that reflect their individual sites. And The Travelling Stone Sauvignon Blanc is produced from vines growing in a sandstone and quartzite mix that is thought to have washed down with the Breede River over thousands of years.

The river is a focal point of the farm. Easy-drinking wines in the River's Edge range come from vines that grow in its alluvial soil and are tended by Weltevrede's farm workers for their own profit (a percentage goes to the Edge of Life Fund, which supports projects such as a local centre for children with learning disabilities). The Breede has also inspired one of the farm's two nature conservation schemes: the protection of its four-kilometre river frontage to ensure the survival of some of the area's oldest known specimens of the rare Breede River yellowwood tree and an endangered fish. In the other scheme, the Jonkers have set aside about 50 per cent of their land as part of the Weltevrede Conservancy, in which pristine renosterveld is protected.

Having established Weltevrede's reputation as a Chardonnay specialist, Jonker intends going one step further and making the farm a dedicated 'champagne house'. His award-winning Philip Jonker Brut, a pure Chardonnay Blanc de Blancs, has been joined by two more bottle-fermented sparkling wines, with a Brut Rosé to come. The names reflect their maker's poetic inclination: The Ring (his first solo effort, which was disgorged for his wedding to Lindelize), Entheos (Greek for spirituality) and Aletheia (Greek for unmasked).

Another of Jonker's personal projects is the excavation of underground concrete tanks that were built in the early 1900s, subsequently hidden beneath a cellar and recently unearthed. A candle-lit tour through the cool, hushed labyrinth of tunnels linking the tanks evokes the romance of European *caves*. Jonker intends developing a self-guided 'tasting route' underground, but for now casual tastings still take place around the old basket press in the wood-panelled tasting room next to the winery.

Breakfasts, teas and light lunches are served outside on a patio beneath a trellised vine at tables decked in cheery red tablecloths. Better still, if you decide to stay overnight, you can enjoy the spectacle of sunset over the vineyards from the *stoep* of either the thatched century-old cottage Ons Huisie or the renovated farmhouse Belvedere.

Not only winemakers, the Jonkers have a strong literary bent too, with third-generation Lourens and Annamarie and fourth-generation Philip and Lindelize all following a line of story tellers who love to read and to write. Lourens is also a director of the publishing group Naspers. The family plans to open The Writer's Studio soon, offering their extensive library as a retreat to writers seeking inspiration, solitude and access to a significant private collection of Africana and other rare books.

details

- 🍷 **Wine tasting/sales:** Mon-Fri 8 am-5 pm; Sat 9 am-3.30 pm. Closed Easter Friday, 25 December and 1 January. Tasting cost: no charge.
- 🛢 **Cellar tours:** by appointment.
- 🍽 **Restaurant:** Friends @ Weltevrede, open Tues-Sat for breakfast and lunch.
- 🏠 **Accommodation:** Ons Huisie (for two) and Belvedere (for a family) self-catering cottages.
- 👪 **Children:** welcome, but no special provision made.
- ⓘ **In addition:** walks (guided by winemaker Philip Jonker by prior arrangement). Mountain bike and 4x4 trails through the Weltevrede Conservancy. Writer's Studio library and writers' retreat.
- ☎ **Tel:** (+27-23) 616 2141.
- 🖱 **Website:** *www.weltevrede.com*

SARONSBERG

Tulbagh

This avant-garde winery, with its
cathedral-like cellar set beneath
its eponymous mountain peak,
serves up some of the Cape's
finest red wines in surrounds
filled with art and music.

A month after a Pretoria businessman had bought two fruit and wine farms in the mountain-ringed valley of Tulbagh in 2002, a fire raged through the orchards and vineyards. Serendipitously, as it turned out, for replanting and building plans were brought forward and out of the ashes rose a state-of-the-art cellar, a modern cathedral to wine in red brick, cement and stone.

Starting with a clean slate and armed with thorough soil analyses, the winery's young viticulturist and winemaker Dewaldt Heyns has been able to exploit specific sites for particular varieties. Mountainside benches of gravel on clay against the Saronsberg and banks of shale above the nearby Klein Berg River are planted to classic red varieties. Shiraz stars, thriving in the shale and coping with the summer heat. It is also Heyns's passion, and appears as acclaimed single-varietal wines or with Mourvèdre, Grenache and Viognier in the award-winning Full Circle Rhône-style blend.

Of the Bordeaux varieties planted, Merlot, Malbec and Petit Verdot do particularly well, adding lustre to the Cabernet Sauvignon-dominated Seismic and Provenance red blends. The name of the former commemorates the earthquake that devastated Tulbagh in 1969. 'Provenance', denoting a whole range of blended wines, reflects the vintner's philosophy of keeping things simple in the cellar to allow the fruit to express itself.

Having driven through Tulbagh – now restored – and out into the hot, dry, somewhat harsh summer landscape, you'll welcome the green of vines, oaks and lawns beside the dam in front of Saronsberg's cellar. Better still is the cool, cavernous tasting room. Floor-to-ceiling steel-paned windows, moss-green velvet armchairs by a central open hearth, and heavy wooden tables juxtaposed with Philippe Starck chairs add up to an unexpectedly rich aesthetic experience. Strains of Gregorian chant or the mellifluous sounds of an instrumental compilation may greet you, and one of those close to the winemaking process – including possibly Heyns himself – will be in attendance. If not, ring for attention; there's a convenient bell on the grand slate-and-granite counter. While you wait, enjoy the modern art and sculpture by leading South African artists displayed here and on the bright, airy mezzanine level. The farm's owner is an avid art collector and among the pieces exhibited is the original artwork for the Provenance label, which was commissioned from Paul du Toit.

The tasting room looks into the fermentation cellar on one side and the dimly lit barrel maturation room on the other. Heyns will be happy to show you around if he isn't busy, but book a tour in advance if you're interested in the finer details of winemaking. The young vintner, recently inducted into the prestigious Cape Winemakers Guild, assisted in the design of the cellar to ensure that the gentle, gravity-fed movement of grapes and wines was accommodated. He delights in being hands on in the cellar, although the appointment of an assistant now frees him up to spend more time in the vineyards too. The grapes are picked and sorted by hand, and small custom-made stainless steel tanks allow for the separate vinification of each one-hectare vineyard block. Thus their individual soil type, clone and variety provide a palette of flavours and styles for blending.

Serious wine lovers should enquire about any future releases or 'experimental' wines that Heyns may have tucked away – perhaps a Brut Cap Classique (the first Pinot Noir and more Chardonnay have been planted for this) or some naturally sweet 'straw' wine. And, although the cellar's reputation rests largely on reds, Heyns's skills come to the fore in the whites too, with an elegant Chardonnay and a particularly zesty Sauvignon Blanc. He also makes the Nick & Forti's range of wines in collaboration with chef Fortunato Mazonne, who runs the Ritrovo restaurant in Pretoria.

Don't miss... joining the gracious steel-and-stone 'lady of the lake' sculpture at the cellar entrance for a glass of wine. Under the oaks and with the Saronsberg peak in the background, it's the perfect spot for the summer lunchtime picnics on the second Saturday of every month.

you'll welcome the green of vines, oaks and lawns beside the dam in front of Saronsberg's cellar

PREVIOUS SPREAD Musical wine lovers are welcome to tickle the ivories of the tasting room's Bernard Steiner baby grand.

Banks of shale on an ancient riverbed produce classic reds.

THIS SPREAD The farm's Bordeaux varieties are planted up against the slopes of the Saronsberg peak, part of the Obiqua range.

Angus Taylor's dam-side '*Uit klip uit water*' sculpture features river stones collected on site.

Winemaker Dewaldt Heyns enjoying a glass of his favourite Shiraz.

An oasis in the heart of the rugged Tulbagh valley.

A cathedral to wine.

The double-volume tasting room, including a mezzanine gallery, displays works by leading South African artists.

details

🍷 **Wine tasting/sales:** Mon-Fri 8 am-5 pm; Sat 10 am-2 pm. Closed public holidays. Tasting cost: R25 (refunded on purchase).

🛢 **Cellar tours:** by appointment.

🧺 **Picnics:** pre-ordered lunchtime picnic baskets on the second Saturday of every month in summer.

👫 **Children:** lawns and a dam; outdoor sculptures provide an impromptu lesson in art appreciation.

ⓘ **In addition:** South African artworks and sculpture.

☎ **Tel:** (+27-23) 230 0707.

🖱 **Website:** *www.saronsberg.com*

RIJK'S
Tulbagh

Set among vines and roses at the foot of the Witzenberg,

Rijk's is a study in simplicity. Yet this young cellar's award-winning

wines have revolutionised red winemaking in the Tulbagh Valley.

With each passing vintage, Wahl assesses the development of character and quality in individual blocks and varieties, with a premium white blend as his ultimate goal

PREVIOUS SPREAD Rijk's tasting room and cellar, set among lush green vines and snow-white Iceberg roses, is a simple but beautiful sight in summer.

THIS SPREAD Neatly demarcated vineyard blocks, home of The Crossing red blend.

Stacking barrels the practical, rather than pretty way.

Picking in the cool pre-dawn captures fresh fruit flavours.

Experience rural peace in the Rijk's Country House suites.

This is hands-on winemaking using traditional methods like manually punching down the red wines in open fermenters.

Rijk's Private Cellar has been doing the unexpected since its inception in 1996, when Capetonian Neville Dorrington bought a stretch of virgin land along the lower slopes of the Witzenberg range in Tulbagh. Against local wisdom, which held that he should plant fruit, he set his sights on vines and particularly red varieties. Scientific analysis showed that the soil, composed of well-drained Malmesbury shale, is eminently suitable. Moreover, in conjunction with a carefully monitored drip irrigation system, it could produce wine with more concentrated flavours. Dorrington subsequently established some 10 varieties in small, micro-managed parcels over some 30 hectares.

Since the success of the farm's maiden vintage, led by Rijk's Pinotage 2000, Dorrington and his young winemaker Pierre Wahl have continued to produce great reds, notably Shiraz and Rhône-like Shiraz blends, epitomised in The Crossing. Wahl has also combined Shiraz with Bordeaux classics Cabernet Sauvignon and Merlot, aptly naming the best bottling Bravado. Being made in small quantities (a few hundred cases), the premium reds are not always available for tasting but they are worth taking home. Having spent up to two years in new French oak, they are then laid down for two to three years and only released when Pierre feels they are ready. As a result, they end up a vintage or two behind the market.

With each passing vintage, Wahl assesses the development of character and quality in individual blocks and varieties, with a premium white blend as his ultimate goal. He has a soft spot for Chenin Blanc and is doing some great things with it in barrel, as he is with Sémillon. Rijk's Sémillon is one of the few varietal examples around, while Fascination is a blend of Sauvignon Blanc and Sémillon. So far, the performance of the farm's Pinotage, Chenin Blanc and Chardonnay has warranted a new Reserve range.

The quality of Rijk's wines is belied by the simplicity of the farm, its cellar and its tasting room. A concrete strip road through the vines leads to a building with clean lines in the modern Cape Dutch style: white walls, green corrugated-iron roof and white sash windows with green trim. A large gravel courtyard is surrounded by a low whitewashed wall lined with Iceberg rose bushes, and a vine-covered pergola frames the green cellar doors that lead into the large tasting room. Inside, the tiled floor and creamy yellow walls are offset by tables and chairs in blond wood and light steel. A fireplace is put to good use in winter when snow lies on the surrounding peaks.

The many small stainless steel tanks in the fermentation cellar are visible through a large glass pane behind the tasting counter. By prior arrangement, the winemaker will take you round the simple set-up that combines technologically advanced equipment with the use of traditional basket presses and manual practices like red-wine pump-downs to ensure soft wines.

The well-informed Lucilia, Rijk's self-appointed Jill-of-all-trades, will guide your tasting. Although it appears quite formal, with wines presented in proper sequence in glasses set out on a numbered tasting sheet, Lucilia gives 'a most unorthodox personal view' of the wines she presents – a view in keeping with the strongly individualistic but fairly laid-back people of Rijk's.

Only the driven, restless Neville Dorrington bucks the trend. His latest venture is a second cellar near his home across the valley that will vinify several adjoining small parcels of especially promising young vines. The winery, its sand-coloured walls and brown wood trim blending in with its surroundings, features an underground barrel room that gives a first-hand view of the remarkable profile of this valley's ancient soils.

details

- **Wine tasting/sales:** Mon-Fri 10 am- 4 pm; Sat 10 am-2 pm. Closed Easter Friday to Monday, 25 December and 1 January. Tasting cost: R5 per wine (refunded on purchase).
- **Cellar tours:** during tasting hours or by appointment.
- **Restaurant:** Rijk's Country House is nearby for breakfast, lunch, dinner and picnics; tel. (+27-23) 230 1006.
- **Functions:** Rijk's Country House for weddings, seminars and small conferences; tel. (+27-23) 230 1006.
- **Accommodation:** at Rijk's Country House, with a pool and a wine bar; tel. (+27-23) 230 1006.
- **Children:** welcome, but no special provision made.
- **Tel:** (+27-23) 230 1622.
- **Website:** *www.rijks.co.za*

MARDOUW
COUNTRY HOUSE
Breede River

A scenic drive from Cape Town takes you to the historic town of Swellendam where, just a stone's throw away, you'll find Mardouw Country House on a pretty olive and wine estate at the foot of the Langeberg range. This Cape Georgian retreat in the Breede River winelands provides a tranquil escape from city life, and combines modern simplicity with historic elegance.

Built 100 years ago as a home for a wealthy local farming family, the Van Eedens, the house has been sensitively restored. Today the accommodation is luxurious, its décor enhanced by the works of renowned South African artists. It provides fireside warmth on cool evenings, while hot days can be spent at the pool. More energetic guests will enjoy a session on the golf driving range or long walks on trails through the surrounding fynbos, with its rich birdlife and magnificent views to the mountains all around. Further afield, there are historic towns and neighbouring wine farms to explore. And when you return to Mardouw, there is no better way to round off the day than to sit on the verandah of your suite and enjoy a glass of wine with *tapas* as the sun sets.

Executive chef Karen ensures that fine dining is the order of the evening, while friendly and efficient staff are keen to attend to your every need. As you return to your suite after an excellent meal, there's a good chance you'll hear the gentle hoot of an eagle-owl or the ethereal chant of a nightjar – the musical signature of Mardouw.

MARDOUW COUNTRY HOUSE (3)

details

How to get there
From Cape Town take the N2 towards Swellendam and, at Stormsvlei, turn left onto the R317. After 16 km, at the Gelukshoop Pad/Drew signpost, turn right and continue for another 15 km. Turn left, cross the Breede River and drive to the R60, turning left towards Ashton. Mardouw is about 2.5 km further along on the right. Alternatively, from Cape Town take the N1 to Worcester and the R60 through Ashton towards Swellendam. Mardouw is about 20 km beyond Ashton, on the left.

Who to contact
Tel. (+27-23) 616 2999, e-mail *reservations@mardouw.com* or go to *www.mardouw.com*

KINGSRIVER
ESTATE GUEST HOUSE

McGregor

Kingsriver Estate, a new gem on the renowned Route 62, lies just a short distance from the pretty village of McGregor and in an area of remarkable beauty and tranquillity in the Langeberg range. Established as a working farm in 1831, it has been restored to its former glory and the original homestead has been converted into a 4-star guest house with three luxury en-suite rooms. A welcoming dining room and a spacious verandah are perfect for relaxed wining and dining, and enjoying a typical Kingsriver 'tavola' experience. Apricot orchards provide seasonal bounty, while a well-stocked herb garden ensures that the chef has fresh flavours right outside the kitchen door.

The surrounding countryside is rich in Karoo vegetation and offers several alternatives for a relaxing outing, whether it is hiking or biking, a day-long picnic or a stroll through vineyards. If you choose the picnic option, a gourmet basket can be delivered to you in secluded caves in the river canyon. Alternatively, visit the restaurant overlooking the vineyards for breakfast, lunch or dinner.

In the McGregor Valley, winter days are often crisp and invigorating, while in summer the heat of the day is tempered by cooling breezes in the late afternoon. At any time of year, an escape to Kingsriver from the stresses of city life is an energising experience, with the calls of the vibrant birdlife a reminder that the beauty of Kingsriver lies in its peace and solitude.

details

How to get there
From Cape Town take the N1 to Worcester, where you join the R62 to Robertson. In Robertson, pass the Shell petrol station and KFC, then turn right towards McGregor. Follow the road and cross the Breede River after 2 km, keeping left towards McGregor. Continue for another 9 km, then turn sharp right at the green sign to Koningsrivier and the brown sign to Trossachs. Follow this gravel road to a T-junction and turn left, continuing until you come to Kingsriver Estate on the right.

Who to contact
Tel. (+27-23) 625 1040, e-mail *kingsriver-guesthouse@breede.co.za* or go to *www.kingsriver-estate.com*

KINGSRIVER ESTATE GUEST HOUSE (3)

RIJK'S
COUNTRY HOUSE
Tulbagh

Nestled in the beautiful Tulbagh Valley, Rijk's Country House is situated on the eminent Rijk's wine farm. With 10 superior rooms, two luxury rooms and three two-bedroomed family suites – each with views of the majestic Witzenberg and Winterhoek mountains – it offers spacious accommodation in a peaceful country setting.

Activities can be as leisurely as you like: swimming in or relaxing by the pool, a gentle game of *boules*, walking among the hundreds of roses or settling down with a book by the fire in the lounge. But there are also opportunities for more strenuous fun: hiking, fishing, birdwatching, horse riding or mountain biking – and even, in summer, helping to harvest grapes by night. And Tulbagh itself, with its incomparable wealth of Cape Dutch and Victorian architecture – Church Street alone has 32 National Monuments – is a fascinating town to explore.

Wine tasting, appropriately enough, is also on Rijk's Country House's list of things to do; head for the Polo Wine Bar and Tasting Room if you wish to sample or purchase wines from the farm. When it comes to meals, you can enjoy international and traditional South African cuisine in the intimate restaurant Que Sera or the private dining room Mon Ami, or you can dine alfresco on the Iceberg Terrace.

The Iceberg roses that are a feature of Rijk's Country House help to make it an ideal venue for weddings. More prosaically, its conference facility can accommodate up to 60 delegates.

RIJK'S COUNTRY HOUSE (3)

details

How to get there
From Cape Town follow the N1 towards Paarl, taking the Klapmuts/Wellington exit to join the R44. Just before Wellington, turn left to Hermon/Ceres, continuing on the R44 through the Nuwekloof Pass, where it becomes the R46. Drive through Tulbagh to a stop street and continue for about 2 km until you reach Rijk's wine farm on the left.

Who to contact
Tel. (+27-23) 230 1006, e-mail *reservations@rijkscountryhouse.co.za* or go to *www.africanpridehotels.com/rijks*

BARTHOLOMEUS KLIP (3)

BARTHOLOMEUS KLIP *Bo-Hermon*

Although it lies within sight of Table Mountain, Bartholomeus Klip is far removed from Cape Town's bustle and offers guests an opportunity to experience country life in the Western Cape. A typical winter's day on the farm could include a brisk walk or bicycle ride through its wheat fields or private fynbos nature reserve, while in summer the old oaks in the garden provide welcome shade and a large dam offers water-borne activities for the more energetic. At any time of year, springbok, eland, zebra and other wildlife can be seen on the twice-daily game drives through the nature reserve, and there are many neighbouring wineries and attractive small towns to explore.

With four rooms and one suite, Bartholomeus Klip accommodates a maximum of 10 guests, which is probably why it is remembered for its homely atmosphere. The typical friendliness of the country people who make up its staff no doubt plays a role too, as do the intimacy of its Victorian farmhouse and the welcoming touches of home-made biscuits and evening sherry in the bedrooms. Exceptional food and a carefully devised wine list are the finishing touches to a memorable stay.

details

How to get there
From Wellington take the R44 to Tulbagh and after 26 km turn right to Bo-Hermon; follow this untarred road for 7 km to the farm.

Who to contact
Tel. (+27-22) 448 1820, e-mail *info@bartholomeusklip.com* or go to *www.bartholomeusklip.com*

AFRICA
Geographic

An Africa Geographic publication

Africa Geographic
1st floor, Devonshire Court
20 Devonshire Road, Wynberg 7800
Cape Town, South Africa
www.africageographic.com

Reg. no. 1992/005883/07
First published 2009

Photographs © David Rogers, or as credited individually
Cover photograph taken at Zorgvliet
Text © Wendy Toerien

Editor Leni Martin
Art Director Bryony Branch
Designer Cindy Armstrong
Project Director Jenni Saunders
Project Manager Tracy Bennett

Reproduction in Cape Town by Resolution Colour (Pty) Ltd
Printed & bound by Tien Wah Press (Pte) Ltd, Singapore

ISBN 978 0 620 43538 3

AFRICA GEOGRAPHIC TRAVEL

Further information on all the estates featured in *Cape Winelands in Style* can be found at the end of each entry. Your local travel agent or consultant should also be able to provide help and advice. Africa Geographic Travel is a full service tour operator and can assist in arranging your travel to the Cape, and further afield in Africa. We specialise in tailor-made itineraries and safaris. Visit *www.africageographictravel.com* for more information.

Africa Geographic Travel
Devonshire Court
20 Devonshire Road
Wynberg 7700
Cape Town, South Africa
Tel. (+27-21) 762 2180
Fax (+27-21) 762 2246
E-mail *travel@africageographic.com*
Website *www.africageographictravel.com*